SEARCHING FOR

NOAH'S ARK

DR. JOHN D. MORRIS

HARVEST HOUSE PUBLISHERS
EUGENE, OREGON

Cover by Knail

Cover photos © Mt. Ararat: Wikimedia Creative Commons; Ark: Karle Horn, Wikimedia Creative Commons; various images from freerangestock.com, freeimages.com, unsplash.com & pexels.com

Photo and image credits: Page 4: John D. Morris; page 6: John D. Morris; page 8: Elfred Lee; page 12: Bigstock; page 14: John D. Morris; page 15: John D. Morris; page 17: John D. Morris; Page 20: John D. Morris; page 26: John D. Morris; page 33: John D. Morris; page 34: John D. Morris; page 35: John D. Morris; page 36: Susan Windsor; page 43: Institute for Creation Research; page 49: Institute for Creation Research; page 56: John D. Morris.

Searching for Noah's Ark
Copyright © 2018 Dr. John D. Morris
Published by Harvest House Publishers
Eugene, Oregon 97408
www.harvesthousepublishers.com

ISBN: 978-0-7369-7319-9 (pbk.)
ISBN: 978-0-7369-7320-5 (eBook)

Printed in the United States of America

18 19 20 21 22 23 24 25 26 / VP-JC / 10 9 8 7 6 5 4 3 2 1

CONTENTS

WHAT HAPPENED TO THE ARK?

The Flood of Noah's day was the greatest cataclysm the world has ever known. For more than a year, waves of water scoured the planet, destroying everything in their path and burying millions of Earth's denizens in thick layers of mud spanning entire continents. All land creatures died—except those aboard the Ark.

The Ark, an immense, barge-like ship, was built by Noah at God's command to preserve the life needed to repopulate the earth once the Flood had accomplished its judgment. After safely bringing its precious cargo through an event violent enough to reshape the planet's entire surface, it came to rest "in the seventh month, the seventeenth day of the month, on the mountains of Ararat" (Genesis 8:4). Having served its purpose, the Ark then disappeared from the Bible's pages.

But what happened to it? Over time, stories emerged of a huge, box-like object spotted on the icy slopes of Mt. Ararat in the wilds of eastern Turkey. Could it possibly be what's left of the Ark? Starting in 1972, Dr. John Morris of the Institute for Creation Research led numerous expeditions to this dangerous part of the world to find out. Here are just a few of the adventures, dangers, and difficulties he and his teams encountered.

4

1

WHY WE SEARCH

August, 1984

The night was absolutely jet black. No light at all other than starlight. We were on the remote Turkish frontier in a sensitive military zone along both the Russian and Iranian borders. We were there to search the imposing Mt. Ararat for any possible remains of Noah's Ark.

Gaining permission from the Turks to search Mt. Ararat posed many problems, but we persevered. We had our permits—almost. We lacked only one signature from the local Gendarme commander. As we waited, all we could do was pray. So around midnight, the night before we were scheduled to begin climbing, after the rest of the climbers had turned in, my coleader and I went walking and praying, desperate for an intervention from God.

A lone Gendarme soldier appeared out of the impenetrable gloom. Screaming, shouting, and shaking, he jabbed his machine gun into my forehead and shoved me face-down in the ditch. He straddled me with his gun pointed directly at the back of my head.

He had his orders. He was trying to shoot me, but had never shot a person before, and killing a man isn't easy. I shouted back as best I could in broken Turkish, but he was just an uneducated peasant from a Kurdish village and knew little Turkish.

He had been told to guard this lonely stretch of road along the militarized border, apprehend any suspicious persons, and shoot them if necessary. He had seen the alert that foreign smugglers were in the area, and were to be shot on sight. To him we were definitely suspicious, walking along a desolate road and speaking a language he couldn't understand. Thankfully, God answers the desperate pleas of His children, and that night, as well as on many other occasions, He answered mine.

Ararat expeditions often result in stories like mine. We've been shot at, thrown in jail, attacked by wild animals, captured by Kurdish terrorists,

and robbed at gunpoint by thieves. We've endured mountaineering perils, disease, and governmental opposition. We were even struck by lightning near the summit, badly injured, and paralyzed for hours. You might ask, "Why continue the search? What could possibly be worth all this?"

Noah's Ark.

Modern and historical eyewitness accounts abound of the remains of a large boat high atop the 17,000-foot peak. Since the 1950s, Westerners have attempted to confirm them. Motivated by these reports, I traveled to Mt. Ararat more than a dozen times and was subjected to some of its most severe punishments and human opposition. Yet the search goes on.

Would the Discovery of Noah's Ark Do Any Good?

Some people think the Ark will never be found, that God would not allow such a discovery because people might worship it or that such obvious evidence would eliminate the need for faith. Others think the Ark has already been found. Still others, including those of us at Institute for Creation Research, think the search should continue, following every lead—both old and new.

Regardless of the chances of finding the Ark, we can only speculate about the results of a successful search—the discovery and documentation of the Ark of Noah, compelling anyone with an open mind to deal with it. The potential good far outweighs the damage an incomplete search would have, for several reasons:

Archaeological. The great Flood of Noah's day, as described in Scripture, would have totally destroyed the surface of the planet. No evidence of civilization could have survived, except perhaps in the form of rare artifacts. Noah's Ark constitutes the one remaining link to the pre-Flood world.

Biblical. No event in Scripture receives ridicule by scientists or doubt by skeptics as much as the Flood and Noah's Ark. Clear evidence would silence the critics of creation science and increase the faith of Christians worldwide.

Scientific. The evolutionary worldview invariably rests on the assumption of uniformitarianism, that "the present is the key to the past." Its basic tenet is that there has never been any episode of Earth history dramatically different from episodes possible today, and that by studying the present we can come to important conclusions about the past. There is no room in this view for a supernaturally caused, mountain-covering, globally devastating flood within human history. To find the Ark atop a high mountain would destroy the concept of uniformitarianism, the basic assumption upon which evolution rests.

Theological. Noah's Flood was a judgment on sin—that of the pre-Flood civilization. God could not and cannot allow sin to go unpunished. Noah's Ark was the means by which the few believers of that day (i.e., Noah and his family) demonstrated their faith and were saved. By calling attention to the past judgment on sin and the past Ark of safety, many minds and hearts could be focused on the coming judgment on sin and our present-day Ark of safety, Jesus Christ.

2
EYEWITNESS ACCOUNTS

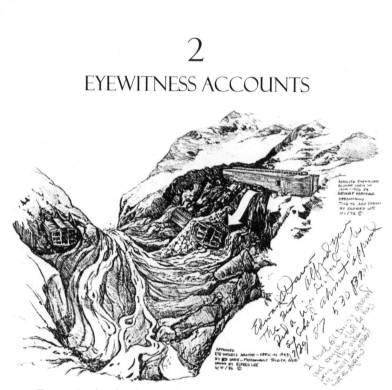

Eyewitness sketch. Image credit: Elfred Lee (used with permission).

As a scientist, I am unwilling to conclude the Ark is there until I see the evidence, but the eyewitness accounts of scores of individuals substantially agree with each other.[1] They describe the Ark in the same general fashion—a large, rectangular barge, usually with a catwalk on the top and a window running its entire length. They likewise describe it as being high on the mountain but not as high as the summit. They generally claim that at the end of a long, hot summer, a portion of it can be seen beneath the snow and rock. Most claim it is in very steep terrain, perhaps on a ledge adjacent to a cliff. For a variety of reasons, no one has been able to pinpoint the location.

Throughout my years of searching, I compiled a brief list of eyewitness accounts.

Table of Eyewitness Accounts

1883	Turkish commissioners checking reports
WW I	Several Armenian Ararat residents
1916	Turkish soldiers returning from World War I
1916	German/Russian Weist family
1916–17	Russian expedition
1917	A Russian expedition takes photos of a box-like object on Mount Ararat; photos later surfaced in 1970 through Russian Armais Arutunoff
1930	American Mark Rafter
1935	American George Greene
1940	Australian soldiers Nice and Tibbets
1943	American soldier Ed Davis
1943	American Vince Will
1945	American Lester Walton
1948	American airman Andy Anderson
1948	Turkish shepherd Resit
1952	American Navy photographer William Todd
1959	American Air Force George Schwinghammer
1969	American Air Force Walter Hunter
1974	American Air Force Ed Behling
1974	US Navy Al Shappell
1985	Air Force General Ralph Havens
1989	US Photo Interpreter George Stephen
1989	Turkish anthropologist Ahmet Arslan

The dangers of Ararat itself presented tremendous obstacles in confirming these accounts, but the political tensions in that area, as well as the suffocating amount of red tape throughout the Turkish government, made the search much more difficult.

The Ararat area has experienced almost constant war for thousands of years. Two of the ethnic groups that lived nearby caused problems in the past, affecting the search for the Ark. The remnant of the Armenian people who lived in Russia within sight of Mt. Ararat called for retribution for the loss of their traditional homeland from which they were driven by the Turks in World War I.

The Kurdish tribes who lived on Mt. Ararat supported, but did not participate in, the civil war in Iraq and Syria raging over the issue of Kurdish independence. Turkey was afraid that the conflict would spread into their country. In both cases, the calling of attention to the Ararat area would have favored the causes of the minorities.

The borders of Turkey, Iran, and the former Soviet state Armenia all converged at the base of Mt. Ararat, forming a perfect storm of political turmoil. Searching for the Ark was not just an easy international flight followed by a quick hike through a beautiful countryside. It required years of dedication and the willingness to endure not just danger but frustration. Rather than climbing Mt. Ararat, most of my time in Turkey was spent driving around trying to get a permit.

Let me tell you one interesting story of an "eyewitness account." On most of our trips, we were limited to searching on foot. One summer, we were granted the use of an aircraft. We were purposively hampered by the military commander in Eastern Turkey until a major summer storm covered the entire mountain. He couldn't even see the mountain that day and thought we would not fly. But we did. Clouds have a lid to them, and above them the mountain was wonderfully clear and visibility was hampered only by the fresh snow (which was too extensive to see anything on the mountain itself). We made no discovery but succeeded in ruling out one possible site and even took some beautiful pictures.

There was a man present who knew little about the search, but as we spent time with him, he caught the bug big time. He went back the next summer. I didn't participate, but helped him plan his itinerary. Imagine my surprise when he called me from Turkey with the news that he had found the Ark! With a helicopter, he had checked a location that none of us had considered, although we had photographed it from a distance. When he called, I got out my photos. Maybe he had found it and our long, grueling search was over. When he returned in September with his videos...maybe. I and other scientists at ICR were intrigued enough to think he may have made a discovery, but the evidence turned out to be insufficient to convince anyone, especially a skeptic.

And so, even though the primary time for searching is August, before the winter snows descend, and this was already September, we set about contacting the proper Turkish officials and raising the necessary money to return immediately. If the Ark was present and visible this year, we wanted to know and observe it. Next year might be too late.

God blessed our efforts and we arrived in Eastern Turkey in October. From a distance we saw the spot up in the glacier. Nothing is ever easy in Turkey, and even though we had acquired the necessary permits, we were again hampered from flying. Time dragged on, and a major storm was approaching. Finally, as dusk was settling on the next day, we were allowed to fly. You can imagine how elated I was as the helicopter took off. Perhaps my long search was over. As we approached, my excitement increased. The others in the helicopter reflected my enthusiasm. But, as we flew perilously close to the side of the mountain, a thought came to mind. After two more passes, I blurted out, "Guys, I'm a geologist and an honest scientist, and that's a rock!" Suddenly everyone could see what I was seeing, and the Ark structure "dissolved" into a cave under a ledge. We had prepared to have the helicopter deposit us at high elevation, but now the value of such a dangerous escapade was waning. Night had fallen and a storm was moving in. Crestfallen, we turned back.

•••••••••••••••••••••••••••

In 1959, a Turkish government map preparer named Ilhan Durpinar supposedly found a boat-shaped object in aerial photographs near Ararat. *Life* magazine reported this in 1960. The boat-shaped object was situated about 20 miles south of Ararat proper at about 7,000 feet in elevation. In

August of that year, a creation scientist launched an expedition to check out the discovery. They concluded that it was simply a natural formation, with the prominent teardrop shape having been eroded by downslope mudslides of volcanic ash and debris. Ark searchers dismissed the report. Then in the early 1980s, an American named Ron Wyatt made the same claim that it was the Ark! Subsequently, I and several others carried out a serious investigation, and we disagreed with his claims.

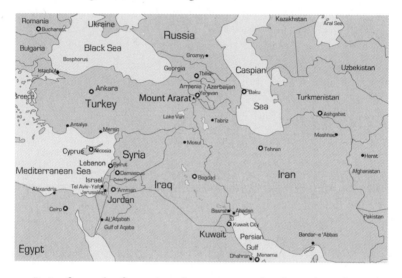

In its favor, the formation does sport a rather boat-shaped appearance. But the shape is so different from all eyewitness accounts of a long barge that it was easy to discount. On several occasions over the subsequent decades, I have returned and studied it carefully. Contrary to Ron Wyatt's claims, there is no petrified wood there, nor are there any metallic rivets, and there is certainly no claimed abnormal carbon count representing animal dung left from the Ark's journey. There is a metallic vein running through the volcanic strata. And local shepherds regularly graze their flock on the site. The teardrop shape came about as a result of the downhill flow of mud being impaled, in a sense, on the one solid rock in the center of the flow path.

3

ROCKSLIDES AND ROBBERY

Mt. Ararat is a volcano, and it has erupted numerous times since the Flood. Its height causes it to be covered by an ice cap that continually erodes the hardened basaltic rock underneath. As the ice sheets move along, they push the loosened rock over the edges of the mountain, causing high-speed avalanches. Often a dislodged boulder will roll like a wheel, screaming like shrapnel. On my first expedition, I was warned about the "crumbly rock" but was not prepared for the enormity of the dangers it imposed.

Thursday, August 3, 1972

> As we talked, I heard a noise up above us on the slope. I looked up just in time to see a basketball-size rock hurtling through the air right at my head, traveling at great speed and only a few feet away. I ducked instantly, and it whistled by just six inches away. We stood in stunned silence for a few seconds until we saw dozens of such rocks speeding toward us from above. We left our packs and ran up the side slopes, off the glacier, and onto the loose rock. (At that point even the loose rock was safer than the glacier.) We watched as these rocks bounced all around where we had been standing, expecting to see our equipment demolished at any second, but the shower was over within a minute and no damage had been done. Roger, J.B., and I

sat there for a while, thanking God for His protection and asking for His guidance.

Once our courage returned, we stepped back onto the glacier. Again the rocks came. But we were watching for them and were up the slope before they reached us. However, one stray rock narrowly missed J.B. The situation was indeed grim. We knew the only way up that slope with such heavy packs was on the glacier. We also knew that to stay on the glacier was very dangerous. Furthermore, we knew that the Lord had called us to do a job, sent us halfway around the world, and protected us all the way. So we claimed that protection, preferring the danger to turning back.

Many more times throughout the day we were subjected to similar rockslides. The slope steepened, causing poor footing and slowing our progress, as well as making it more difficult to avoid the slides.

At one point, the side slope that provided us some protection dwindled down to very little. I raced up this small slope once to avoid a slide, but the rocks continued to fall all around me. I ripped off my pack, threw it down, and began dodging, running, jumping, falling, and praying, trying to avoid the rocks. It's very hard to be nimble-footed on these loose rock slopes, especially when wearing metal crampons. But the Lord was in complete control, and I escaped without a scratch, even though many large rocks passed within inches.

The rocks varied from walnut-sized to Volkswagen-sized, but at such dizzying speeds even the small ones could kill. We developed a keen awareness of rockslides weeks earlier in the Ahora Gorge, but these slides were vastly different. They make very little noise in the snow but fall with such force that they shake the earth. The speeds probably reach 100 mph. The rocks' bounces are unpredictable, and it is hard to get out of their way. As they fall, they fly through the air sometimes for hundreds of feet, spinning like a wheel and whistling like shrapnel. Each rock is like a buzz saw and would destroy anything in its path, but we felt we were in the Lord's will and continued climbing the slope.

There were, of course, other dangers on Ararat. The packs of Kurdish wolfhounds that prowled around the mountain were vicious. These animals were bigger than German shepherds, and ugly.

I learned years later that the formal name for the
Kurdish wolfhound is the Anatolian shepherd.

During my first expedition, I was climbing in the Ahora Gorge when my coworker and I were surrounded and attacked by more than ten of these wolfhounds. We each grabbed a rock and tried to scare the dogs away, but the pack closed in—like wolves. Several drooled and foamed at the mouth. They were ready for blood.

Thankfully, the Lord demonstrated His providence, and a Kurdish shepherd showed up and started beating them with a long, thick shepherd's staff. Apparently three of the dogs were his own. With a brief thanks to the stranger, we started off at a fast walk, thanking God for His protection.

The following events on Ararat happened to the climbers in my group, and I recorded them in my diary. There were five of us on this trip in 1972, and at one point we split up. Two of us (J.B. and I) stayed at the camp to do research, and the other three (Roger, Skip, and Bill) went up the mountain, carrying most of our gear. The three of them were traveling with a pair of Kurdish shepherds and camped for the night at the foot of a glacier.

Saturday, August 12, 1972

> Late that night, they were awakened by the sound of a nearby gunshot. They heard several people moving outside, and then a whole volley of shots rang out, followed by much shouting and more shots. Roger sat up and shouted back that they had permission from their friends in the Gendarme to climb, but as he talked a bullet ripped through the tent, narrowly missing his head. He shouted for them to stop and crawled out. Immediately three men surrounded him, jabbing him with their gun barrels and hitting him with clubs while shining a flashlight in his face. Skip and Bill followed and received the same treatment. As they were herded out onto the rocks, all three felt that the end was near.
>
> One of the men, an older man, was extremely harsh and cruel, and as he appeared to be preparing to kill them, Skip and Roger and Bill prayed for him and the others because it was obvious that Satan was in control of their lives and

they needed Jesus Christ and His salvation desperately. One of the thieves was moved by this and restrained the older man from shooting and from any more harsh treatment. He guarded the three climbers while the older man and the third man ransacked the tent, taking everything they could carry. When the thieves left, the only things they left behind were the sleeping bags, the tent, the ice axes, and their boots. These were the only items necessary for survival and retreat back down the mountain. Nothing more could be done that night, so the three men went back to sleep.

The value of the stolen gear was about $3,000, and that was more than 40 years ago. We reported the robbery to the Turkish commander, who promised to look for the gear and bring the thieves to justice. However, we had little hope this would happen.

When we left Turkey, we were satisfied that the loss of our equipment had been allowed by God and that we would never see it again. But as God's providence would have it, three months later, the night before Thanksgiving, our gear was delivered to my house.

4

INTERESTING ARARAT STORIES

I had many adventures in Ararat, on and off the mountain. As I said before, it's a dangerous place, with rebellious Kurds, wild dogs, and unstable politics. Here are just a few of the hundreds of stories I could tell.

Thieves in the Dark

One time, several of us were in Turkey doing preliminary reconnaissance and planning. We were exhausted and got a room at a "hotel" (for lack of a more appropriate term) we had stayed at before. There was no other option. Unfortunately, the water system never worked well, and this time it was totally broken. The toilets didn't work, and the smell was palpable.

We decided to spend the night in our van. I had seen a spot on the desolate donkey trail away from any nearby village and hoped no one would notice if we parked there. We arrived after midnight with no lights at all—no lamps, no moon, nothing. We got as comfortable as we could in the cramped quarters.

Several hours later, with snores coming from the others, I suddenly woke up. I had no sense of foreboding but shone my flashlight outside, just to be safe. Suddenly, as my light brightened the area, shouts came from all directions. My crew awoke and instantly our flashlights were trained outside. There were several men surrounding our vehicle. They must have seen us arrive from a distant vantage point and figured we were an easy mark. Typically the Kurds always carry a rifle or shotgun at night and also pack a wicked knife. Undoubtedly they were thieves, but probably would have gone so far as to slit our throats if we challenged them. Rather than confront them, we drove away quickly, sneaking away in the dark.

The "Wheeler Dealer"

On one occasion we made friends with a local Kurd whom we hoped would be of help with logistics around Ararat. In some ways he was a help, but primarily he was a wheeler dealer, always looking for a way to make a buck and always getting us in trouble. One day he tried to sell us trinkets—rather orthodox Christian icons of Mary and such—that he had taken from Armenian graveyards. We weren't interested. In desperation, he agreed to show us antiquities and took us to an ancient city and cemetery halfway up the mountain—a place normally seen only by the local villagers and graveyard thieves. The ruins obviously were quite old, from the time of the Armenian heyday, but we had things far more ancient on our minds.

On one occasion, he helped me make a film along with a Christian television group from the Netherlands. He took us to various locations on the mountain, but then passed us on to another guide. In one village, a man confronted us with an aimed and loaded shotgun! He took us at gunpoint to the police headquarters at the nearby city of Doğubeyazit, about 40 miles away. Our filming escapade was over, but darkness was approaching anyway. Unknown to me, the filmmaker from Holland was carrying a diplomatic passport. In Turkey, that's like a get-out-of-jail-free card. As soon as he showed it to the police, they let us go, and we walked to our nearby hotel. The villager who had brought us in ended up having to do a long walk back home that night.

The Elderly Couple

In 1983, a ruthless fanatic Muslim dictator came to power in Iran, and he hated America, which he viewed as being "the Great Satan." He was in the process of purging all people he didn't approve of, including Muslims of any other sect. That summer, we were granted permits through proper channels but were waiting for the last signature from the local military commander in Doğubeyazit, the city closest to the Iranian border.

We were scheduled to start climbing at dawn, and two of us were stuck after midnight in the crude police station with my Muslim interpreter, a local man. The only others present were an old peasant-looking couple across the room. After a long while, our interpreter went over to meet with them and help pass the time until the police chief returned. They talked for a few minutes, and suddenly he and they began wailing and crying. He came running over to me and asked for our money. I gave all I had, about $50, to him, and he then gave it to them. Soon the police chief returned. He signed our permit, and as we left, our Muslim interpreter was able to tell us about the old couple.

They had been wealthy owners of a carpet factory in Iran, and even though they were committed Muslims, were affiliated with another party—at that time, the "wrong" party. They had seven sons, all married with large families. That morning the police had asked all seven sons to come in for questioning, and that afternoon the police had returned to the carpet factory with seven body bags and a letter written to the old couple warning them to be out of the country by morning. So here they were at the Turkish police station in the city nearest to the Iranian border with no money, no family, no business, no possessions, and no hope. We left, not knowing what else to do for the wailing couple.

Ishak Pasha Palace near Doğubeyazit in Turkey.

Old Muslim Castle

East of the city of Doğubeyazit is a fabulous ruin of an old Muslim castle designed many years ago by a brilliant Armenian architect for an Arab sheik. It was so ornate that to ensure no one else enjoyed such beauty ever again, the sheik had the hands of the architect chopped off! The castle has stood in ruins since World War I.

On my first trip to Turkey in 1971, I visited the ruins, and they are beautiful. Built with imported rose-red rocks that were ornately carved, I was captivated. We had to climb some distance in the snow to reach the ruins. While exploring around, I came across a series of small rooms somewhat similar to one another, and concluded that this was probably where the sheik had kept his harem.

Hollywood and Leonard Nimoy

Over the years, Hollywood has produced a few movies about the search for the Ark. The first came out in 1973 and was titled *In Search of Noah's Ark*, starring Leonard Nimoy of *Star Trek* fame. I wanted to meet him. Financiers felt the search was of sufficient interest that the movie couldn't fail. I was asked to help as a consultant on the script and to be in the movie to talk about my adventures on my first expedition. I was quickly introduced to the fact that in Hollywood, there's not a lot of emphasis on accuracy. "Evidence" for the Ark was introduced that I knew wasn't true, but this mattered little to the producers. The fledgling satellite photography in existence in the day had found an "anomaly." I knew where they were pointing. It was a tin-roofed building on Ararat's lower slopes. Other similar mistakes were committed, but why should they care?

However, I learned one thing of value. In the mountains of Utah, the producers had a wooden replica of the Ark built to the proper dimensions. When they pointed it out to me from a trail, I couldn't see it. Based on that, I realized that evidently an object the size of Noah's Ark *can* disappear. Hollywood made a sequel a decade later, but while it was a financial success, it didn't help the cause. Nor did I ever get to meet Leonard Nimoy. They simply wrote his lines, and he read them in a studio.

Would a Bribe Help?

Over the years of searching, some suggested that I use bribery in the face of all the opposition I experienced. I have been tempted to do so—not only by my own weakness, but also because Turkish officials hinted that a little would perhaps "grease the skids" a bit. But two factors prohibit such choices for me. One is that Scripture strictly disallows bribery (see, for example, Exodus 23:8 and Proverbs 17:23). So God would not bless such an effort. Secondly, while bribery is widely practiced in Turkey, Turkish law levies heavy prison terms (or worse) on those who are caught. Those who have spent time in Turkish prisons would not recommend employing that route. I have been incarcerated only briefly by the Turks, but that one experience was enough for me.

As an alternative, I would offer rewards for information (sometimes that helped) or offer to pay a person's expenses. When I lobbied an official for permission and protection, I knew that his effort would cost the military money. And so I offered, up front, to underwrite the cost. Sometimes this was helpful, but I had no control over how the official used the money after I paid him.

The Novices

I have been to Hong Kong several times for speaking trips. During one visit there, I met with a local group of novice climbers and adventurers who thought they should go to Mt. Ararat on their own. I counseled them on why this was a poor idea, and eventually they all came to the Institute for Creation Research for more preparation. They had a plan to build a Noah's Ark theme park in Hong Kong, the planning for which I got heavily involved. But when they arrived in Turkey, unable to speak the language, a local charlatan (well-known to Ark search veterans) found them easy prey. They had trusting hearts and money to burn. The charlatan hired some villagers to build an Ark façade and allowed the visitors from Hong Kong to "discover" it. In short, they lost a lot of money and produced a Christian theater-quality movie that convinced no one regarding their find.

Turkish Bath

In April 1987, we flew to Turkey to make preparations for our search that coming fall. In particular, we sought the use of a helicopter. While there, we had some free time and decided to visit a Turkish bath. I recorded the (ahem) *interesting* experience in my diary:

> While in the city streets, we decided that this would be a good time to introduce ourselves to an important part of Turkish culture: the Turkish bath, the hamam. So we went back to the hotel and changed our clothes and left most of our money. After receiving instructions from Orhan in what to expect and how to act, we walked over to the Yenishir Hamam.
>
> There was a price for entering the bath, which was about 1,200 Turkish lira. Several individuals, however, worked in the bath unpaid and expected tips from those whom they served. This meant the cost would go up even more.
>
> As we entered, we were shown to a room with a lock. We were to leave our clothes and valuables there and were each given a towel with which to enter the bath. Of course, I was not wearing my glasses by this time and had only a vague understanding of what was going on around us.
>
> The entrance to the bath was already one floor beneath street level, and the bath itself was down another long flight of stairs quite far under the ground. When we arrived at the bath, I thought I knew what to expect because I had read articles about Turkish baths, but I was totally unprepared for the experience. It consisted mainly of a huge sauna with large heated marble slabs on which to lie. One could only lie on the very outside of the slab because the inside was extremely hot—hot enough to burn skin. Until we figured that out, we were most uncomfortable. The slabs are heated by an internal system of gas jets and steam.
>
> The sauna was quite relaxing; we laid there for probably 30 minutes perspiring profusely while the "dirt" on us was loosened. Each of us had a plastic dish on which to lay our heads, and we were clothed only in our towels. I used this 30 minutes to think of upcoming appointments and to pray diligently for success in them. I wondered if this was perhaps one of the few times when

fervent Christian prayer had been offered to God from an Islamic Turkish bath.

My experience from that point onward defies description. As best as I can explain it, I was "attacked" by a man with a Brillo Pad. After he worked me over, I was variously pummeled by four other men in an experience which best is approximated by a drive-through car wash.

More explicitly, the main "attacker," a man named Hasta (the Turkish word for "sick," coincidentally), wore a large glove made out of goat hair. It was extremely rough and was intended to remove all dirt from a person's body. He made quite a point of showing me the dirt that he had rubbed off my arms and chest, but I am convinced he was rubbing off my top layer of skin. He pulled and yanked and scraped while I attempted to maintain an air of aloof disinterest. That was quite impossible under the circumstances.

After scraping me all over for about 15 minutes, from my nose to my toes, excluding certain private parts, he then produced what appeared to be a balloon or pillowcase full of something. Not having seen what had happened to my friends, I had no clue as to what this was. Hasta held this over my head and, all of a sudden, opened it, releasing a large amount of soapy suds to drown me inside and out. He then proceeded with the second round of Brillo-Pad scraping.

After this part was over, a bucket of ice-cold water was poured all over my red-hot body. Intermittent loads of hot and cold buckets entertained me for the next few minutes until I was moved to another bench area next to a stool with hot and cold running water on it. Here we proceeded to go through another series of dowsings, including a shampoo and perhaps crude chiropractic treatments. I'm not sure. All the while, Hasta was telling me to do things, and I had no idea what he was saying.

Finally, Hasta indicated he was finished. He left me to sit there pondering what to do next. I walked out with my dripping-wet towel to another lobby area as I had seen other dim figures do, and there I was attacked by several other men who rubbed me with various towels and wrapped them around me—including on my head. By the time they ushered me out of that chamber, I was wearing, I think, three or four towels.

Similar treatment was afforded me at least one more time, and then I was on my way back up the stairs. Once again I was treated to a rubdown and a change of towels.

Then suddenly the entire experience was over, and I was told to go back to my room and get dressed. Thankfully, I had been able to hang onto my key through all of this. Although I did lose the key momentarily at one point because I didn't have my glasses and I couldn't see. I had to feel all around the hot marble slab to find it.

While I was glad to have experienced a Turkish bath, I was also glad to be all done. I must say I certainly felt clean by the time I left that place.

But the ordeal was not quite over yet. Before we could leave, we had to pass by the array of attackers that had pummeled us in the bath below. Each expected a sizeable tip for what he had done. I suppose in a way they had earned it. Orhan had told us that this would be the case and we were prepared with money to give them, although I could barely recognize those who had participated and am certain I tipped several workers whom I had not seen before.

All in all, the experience was not entirely unpleasant, and I may, if I lapse into insanity, attempt another visit to a hamam at some future date.

5

LIGHTNING STRIKES

Thursday, August 3, 1972
Near the summit of Mt. Ararat
13,000 feet

The snow was falling harder, sliding down the slope, covering our knees as we climbed. The wind was blowing hard, and it was difficult to see. We stopped under a big rock that provided us a little shelter from the wind. Because it was 1:00 p.m., we broke out our trail food. As we ate, Roger dropped his sunglasses, and they fell down a hole at his feet. As he reached after them, he discovered that the hole went on forever. As it turned out, we were standing on a thin ice covering over a large crevasse where the rock and ice separated. Needless to say, we moved.

Because the snow was coming down in such torrents, and we were on the steepest part of the glacier, we decided to rope up, cross the finger glacier to the other side, and continue our ascent on the rocky-side slope. The rocks were almost completely covered with freshly fallen snow and were much more stable than before.

As we persevered, we felt as though we were in the middle of a war. It seemed that Satan was doing his best to destroy us, but God was protecting us. I had felt that on this day we would find the Ark, and it seemed as if Satan was desperately trying to stop us. After all, such a discovery would have a tremendous impact on the world. In spite of the stormy conditions, we were filled with genuine peace. We knew that no matter how tough the going got, the Lord was protecting and leading us. Nothing could happen unless the Lord allowed it to happen. We were in His will and on His mission, and we knew that whatever happened, it would be according to His purpose. How wonderful it is to be a Christian and know that you are right where God wants you.

The weather got worse. The temperature dropped, the wind blew harder, and the snow became thicker. We were on a slope that was at about a 45-degree angle, and when we were only 100 feet below the ridge where we had planned to make camp, thunder clapped all around us and lightning struck nearby. In fact, lightning struck the large rocks all around us repeatedly.

This was the first time I had ever been in a storm—I mean *in* a storm. We were in the clouds. Lightning was not striking in bolts; it was collecting at one place or another. The thunder was deafening all around us. Static electricity was evident everywhere. Our ice axes and crampons were singing, our hair was standing on end, even J.B.'s beard and my moustache were sticking straight out. We could feel the electricity build up until it collected on some nearby rock.

In our training, we had been taught to avoid electrical storms if at all possible, but if ever caught in one, to try to stay away from large rocks. The storm had come upon us quickly, and we were surrounded by big rocks and just below a ridge of huge rocks. Our only hope of safety was to continue upward over the ridge and onto the relatively flat glacier above, yet we had to stay close enough to big rocks so that we ourselves would not be struck directly by lightning.

Although we were in a most dangerous situation, I felt that we would not be struck. I knew that God was allowing the storm but protecting us, and that if we kept our faith in Him, with His help, we would overcome the situation.

The wind and snow kept increasing as we moved upward. At one point, J.B. sat down beneath a large rock to gain some relief from the blinding snow. I had seen lightning strike this rock several times and went back to warn him. It was no use yelling through the wind and snow, so Roger and I took the risk and worked our way toward J.B. But as all three of us stood or sat on this big rock, lightning struck it again, sending unbelievable bolts of electricity through us.

J.B. was frozen to the rock by his back. His arms and legs and head were extended out into the air. He could feel electricity surging through his body. From his suspended vantage point, however, he could see Roger and me thrown off the rock. The force of the lightning seemed to suspend us in the air and then dropped us far down the slope. At this point, J.B. succeeded in forcing one of his legs to the ground, completing the electrical circuit, and the force somersaulted him down the mountain as well, toward Roger and me.

I had been standing on the rock (now known as Zap Rock) when the lightning struck. Once again, I had been thanking the Lord for protecting us, feeling that we would not be harmed. When the bolt struck, my whole body went numb and I could not see or move, but I never lost consciousness. I fell over backward, still wearing my heavy backpack. I expected an impact, but it never came; it seemed like I was floating in the air very slowly for several seconds. I was gently lain on the snow by unseen hands and began sliding down the steep slope. I knew I had to find a way to stop, yet for an instant my eyes and arms would not function. When they did, I spied and grabbed a boulder in the snow, stopping my slide.

For a few seconds I lay there, not moving, aware only of intense pain. I reasoned that because the pain was so great I must have received the full force of the bolt and that the other two men were unaffected. I tried to roll over and sit up, but to my horror found that both my legs were paralyzed. There was no sensation of touch or life in them—just burning, searing pain.

I called to my friends for help, thinking they were unharmed, but the only answer was another call for help. Looking back uphill, I saw J.B. sitting up in the snow, about ten feet away, obviously also in great pain, with one leg twisted underneath him. He also was paralyzed and thought that his twisted leg was broken.

We remained there for some minutes, crying out to God for relief from the pain and deliverance from the horrible death that surely was to be ours. Suddenly I realized I hadn't seen Roger, so I called out to him and frantically looked around for him. J.B. spotted him much farther down the mountain, lying face-down in the snow, one side of his head covered with blood. We were unable to go to him, so we prayed for him and called to him from above. Finally he stood up, looked around, and walked up to us. His face was at least as white as the snow, and his eyes were filled with confusion and fear. He did not come all the way to J.B. and me, but from a few feet away, he bombarded us with questions. "Where are we? What are we doing here? Why don't we go sit under that big rock and get out of this snow?" J.B. patiently tried to explain to him that we were on Mt. Ararat, looking for Noah's Ark, and that we had just been struck by lightning under that big rock.

Roger was in shock and experiencing total amnesia. He didn't know who he was, who we were, or anything else. Furthermore, he didn't even like us. He wondered who these two nuts were sitting in the snow, freezing to death, when they could gain some shelter from the storm up among the rocks. J.B. convinced Roger to go get our ice axes, but that was the only thing he would do to help.

So J.B. and I, unable to help ourselves, had to rely totally upon God. We reasoned that Roger would slip into deeper shock soon and would need medical attention. J.B. thought his leg was broken, and both of us were paralyzed, unable to move. We discussed attempting to descend the mountain, but ruled that out as impossible.

Our situation was, in short, critical. Unless we were able to get to some shelter, we would die within a few hours, freezing to death in the storm. And so, not being able to see any way to alter the situation, I prepared to die.

That's a weird feeling, rationally knowing that you are about to die. I never once doubted my salvation, and I did not fear death. In fact, I felt genuine peace, knowing that soon I was to be with my Savior in heaven. I had always envisioned meeting Jesus face to face as a rather exciting experience, but I now felt no excitement, just comfort. In fact, I wanted to get on with it—to die immediately rather than slowly over a period of hours.

As I sat there contemplating the horrible death that lay in store for me, the Holy Spirit began to interject some of His thoughts into my mind. First, I was reminded of the hundreds of thousands of past Christians who had suffered and died while following the Lord's leading and how they considered it a privilege to suffer for Him. Then I was reminded of the marvelous way in which our group had been led over the past months and particularly the past weeks in Turkey. I was reminded of the miraculous acquisition of our VW minibus, of the Christian friends who had helped us, of the granting of the impossible-to-obtain permits, of the many dead-end streets down which we had wandered only to find an open door at the end. I was reminded of the Christians back home who were praying for our safety and success. I was reminded of the job we had been called to do and its implications, importance, and urgency.

And then the conclusion: No, we weren't going to die. God still had a purpose, a job for us to accomplish. He wasn't going to let us die in that frozen wasteland. Somehow He was going to remedy the situation, heal and strengthen our bodies, and allow us to continue the search for the Ark.

I was then reminded of two passages of Scripture: James 5:15, which states that "the prayer of faith will save the sick," and 1 John 5:14-15, which says, "This is the confidence that we have in Him, that if we ask anything according to His will, He hears us. And if we know that He hears us, whatever we ask, we know that we have the petitions that we have asked of Him."

These thoughts were whirling around in my mind at dizzying speeds. I then knew I wasn't going to die, that I was going to be healed. I knew that this was according to God's will. And I knew that if I prayed with faith, God would hear me. So with my heart pounding wildly, I prayed, knowing that the Lord would hear me and that He would answer my request and heal my body.

Before the Holy Spirit had redirected my thinking, I had prayed for relief from the pain. But it was a prayer of desperation, not of faith. This time I expected a miracle. I tried to move my legs—no response. Or did that toe move? Frantically I began massaging my legs and could feel the firmness return. There was no sensation of touch in them, just a burning numbness. Before when I had felt them, they resembled a balloon filled with water, shapeless and pliable. But now they had firmed up. I continued to massage my legs, covering them with snow to ease the burning sensation. Their strength gradually returned, but I still had no feeling in them. After about 30 minutes, I was able to bend my knees. And within an hour, I was able to stand!

Using an ice axe as a cane, I hobbled over to J.B. and massaged his legs. He had been unable to reach his ankle and still thought it was broken. We determined that it was not broken, but both of his legs felt like jelly. By this time he was quite calm and relaxed, and he felt that Roger needed attention more than he.

Roger was sitting on a nearby rock, obviously cold and still in shock. He didn't even have the sense to put on heavier clothing. So I retrieved his pack and redressed him—nylon pants, down parka, wind parka, and poncho. As I was tying his poncho up around his chin, a look of recognition flickered across his face, and his memory began to return. When he asked why I was dressing him, I knew he was going to be all right. He did not fully recover for several hours, but in the meantime he was able to heat some water for a hot drink. In doing so, we lost all of the coffee, cocoa, tea, soup, all hot drink material. It slid down the slope, along with some valuable equipment.

J.B. had been massaging and flexing his legs all this time. His right leg had recuperated somewhat, and he could move it. Roger and I helped him don warmer clothing and find shelter from the storm.

Finally, I began to dress myself. My legs were weak and shaky. I had walked up and down the slope, gathering gear, until I was exhausted; but together we huddled under the rock to gain shelter from the storm...and prayed to gain victory over the situation.

Earlier, the Holy Spirit had given me the knowledge that it was in the Lord's will for us to be healed and to survive the ordeal. Now we were partially healed and growing stronger each minute, but we still faced a cruel blizzard with little chance of survival. Lightning was still flashing everywhere, snow was still coming down in buckets, and gale-force winds were blowing. We knew we were going to survive, but that making it through the storm wouldn't be easy.

We, as Christians, are expected to have faith—large amounts of it, in fact. But we must never expect our faith to be sufficient. Frequently the Lord requires hard work and then rewards our faith by blessing our efforts. Such was the case on the mountain. We thought the only possible area of safety was on top of the ridge away from the big rocks. We needed a flat place to pitch the tent to get out of the storm, so as soon as the intensity of the lightning strikes lessened, Roger and I began searching for a way to the top.

The wind was blowing the snow so hard we could not see more than ten feet maximum, but we located a path between several huge rocks and climbed it. It was nearly vertical, and footing was treacherous. Once we reached the top, however, we found the weather worse. We were right on the edge of a major glacier, and the wind velocity doubled, but we picked out a flat place to camp and returned to J.B.

While we had been scouting out a place for the tent, J.B. had been massaging and exercising his legs. His right leg had regained its strength, but he still had no response from his left leg. He still could not move, so Roger and I climbed the slope with our packs and made plans to anchor the rope to a rock and assist J.B. in his ascent. I was nearly exhausted after this second climb. My legs were shaking like rubber, so I rested in the snow for several minutes. We descended once again to J.B., and much to our surprise found him standing up, waiting for us. His legs still had no feeling, but their strength had returned enough to allow him to stand, so Roger carried his pack and, with a little assistance from me, he climbed that vertical slope on two numb and weak legs!

Within minutes of reaching the top, the storm broke. I guess the Lord figured that we had had enough. The snow and wind stopped, and the clouds disappeared just as suddenly as they had appeared. In complete comfort and peace, we were able to pitch our tent and eat a hot supper.

In fact, that evening before the sun went down, it was rather warm and pleasant.

Throughout the day, I had felt that this would be the day we would find the Ark. This feeling was strengthened by the fact that it seemed as if Satan was truly determined to stop us. It's not hard to imagine what I was doing and thinking as we pitched the tent and set up camp. As soon as time permitted, I wandered off to the edge of the Ahora Gorge, positive that the Ark was in full view. I did not approach any dangerous cliffs, but with my binoculars I searched in all directions from a safe vantage point. Much to my disappointment, I did not see the Ark, but the view of the gorge from above was magnificent. The freshly fallen snow covered everything above 9,000 feet, including, I suspected, the Ark. So we had to settle for a comfortable place to sleep, hot food, and our lives that night. We were satisfied and gave thanks to God. Very few people have ever camped that high on Ararat, and I'm sure no one else has had such a wonderful time of prayer and singing as we had that evening.

6
ARCHAEOLOGICAL DISCOVERIES

We never found the Ark. While this was disappointing, the discoveries we made along the way added to our knowledge of the history of Ararat that, in addition to a few good stories, at least made our scientific efforts worthwhile.

On multiple expeditions, we investigated a cave in some cliffs near an ancient abandoned castle. Climbers must scale a vertical cliff for 30 feet or so to reach it. Two men with turbans and staffs are carved on either side of its entrance. Above the opening is a carving of a four-legged animal, but its head has eroded beyond recognition. Scholars studying these carvings have determined that the cave was from a civilization older than the Hittites. I was accompanied on one of these expeditions by seasoned climber and photographer Larry Ikenberry and Dr. Jim Davies. Inside, we went down a narrow opening to an area that looked like a foyer, where we saw the broken remains of what appeared to be a coffin. The cave walls had been chiseled out of the rock, and in some places the walls were quite smooth—someone had spent a lot of time carving and polishing them.

In 1972 we visited Korhan, an ancient site of worship. Near the top of a foothill, a large rock-hewn altar was discovered. It was associated with both pictorial writing and an ancient style of cuneiform, more pictorial in form than Sumerian cuneiform and even more ancient. Many other structures and remains were discovered. Surrounding the altar at the very summit of the hill were approximately 25 sacrificial pits, which were used perhaps by later civilizations or lesser personages than those who used the main superbly constructed one. An ancient Armenian graveyard was located nearby with ornate carvings and crosses on the tombstones. Either a large washbasin or a key-base for a statue was nearby. Crosses and carvings were also discovered on the walls of the huge shrine at the base of the hill. Was this from a civilization of Noah's early descendants?

The cave and artifacts mentioned here were formed by ancient inhabitants near where the Ark might have landed. In the region of Ararat there are many such sites and artifacts. Perhaps someday these sites can be examined more closely so we can learn more about the early civilizations that sprang up after the Flood.

7

EVIDENCE FROM HISTORY AND THE BIBLE

Many times and in many ways, the Bible specifies the Flood was global and could be understood only as global. When you read through the pertinent chapters of Genesis, you will repeatedly read of the global nature of the Flood. While it is true that some seemingly all-inclusive words that appear in the Flood narrative can also be used in a more limited sense, proper interpretation depends on the context. For example, the word translated "all" as in "*all* the high hills" (Genesis 7:19) also finds usage in Genesis 41:56-57, where we read that "the famine was over *all* the face of the earth...So *all* countries came to Joseph in Egypt to buy grain, because the famine was severe in *all* lands." Yet far-flung nations on other continents are probably not included. The context in this passage suggests "all" is used in a limited sense, but what of Genesis 7:19 and the rest of the Flood narrative?

Consider that a double superlative precedes "all" in the Hebrew script of Genesis 7:19. The Flood is said to have "prevailed exceedingly" over the earth. By using powerful military imagery, Scripture eliminates the possibility of a limited usage for "all" in this case. If we let the biblical context define its own words, we can come to no other interpretation than that gained from a plain-sense understanding. These terms are meant to be understood in a global sense.

In the Flood chapters, Genesis 6–9, numerous terms are used that normally imply a global phenomenon. Together they provide the context for all the others. Reading them in list form provides a stunning awareness of Scripture's meaning and demands a global interpretation of the whole (see Appendix C).

The account makes no sense if the Flood was local but reads naturally and logically if the Flood was global. How much more clearly could a global flood be described? It would seem that the author of Genesis could hardly have been more explicit. Conversely, if the omniscient Author had intended to describe a local flood, then He obscured the facts. If words can communicate truth, and if God can express Himself clearly, then the Flood was global.

Certainly Jesus Christ, the person of the Godhead intimately involved in accomplishing creation, would know the extent of the Flood. While on Earth, He referred to the Flood in terms best understood as implying its global nature.

Jesus even based His doctrine of the end times on this. While instructing His disciples regarding the last days, He said, "As it was in the days of Noah, so it will be also in the days of the Son of Man: They ate, they drank, they married wives, they were given in marriage, until the day that Noah entered the ark, and the flood came and destroyed them all" (Luke 17:26-27).

Jesus based His teaching of future worldwide judgment on past worldwide judgment and reminded His listeners that the great Flood of Noah's day was global in scope—that it "destroyed them all" (verse 27). By comparing the two episodes, Jesus made it clear that the coming judgment will destroy "all" who are not covered by Christ's sacrificial work on their behalf (i.e., in the Ark of safety, Jesus Christ), just as the past judgment destroyed "all" who refused God's protection in the Ark of Noah.

But what if the Flood was local and destroyed only some rather than all of the world's inhabitants? Christ's teaching would be severely weakened. A global flood implies a coming judgment upon all, not some, while a local flood implies a partial judgment to come. Thus, Christ bases His theology upon a global interpretation of the Flood.

In a similar fashion, Peter reminded his readers that "the world that then existed perished, being flooded with water" (2 Peter 3:6), and bases on it his doctrine of the coming time when the entire "heavens and the earth which are now" will "pass away with a great noise, and the elements will melt with fervent heat; both the earth and the works that are in it will be burned up" (verses 7, 10). He likens the coming destruction and renovation of the entire planet—indeed, the entire universe producing the "new heavens and a new earth" (verse 13)—to the past destruction and renovation of the entire earth.

We might ask those who advocate the local flood theory, "Will the coming re-creation of the new earth be just a local re-creation?" Will it only concern the portions of Earth in which man sins? How does the local flood concept not imply that only part of the earth is "reserved for fire" (verse 7)? Will some sinners actually escape God's coming wrath? Holding the view that the flood was merely local leads to doctrinal nonsense.

One of the strongest evidences for a global flood is the presence of flood legends in the folklore of people groups from around the world. The stories are all remarkably similar. Local geographical and cultural distinctives may be present, but all these accounts seem to be telling the same story.

Over the years I've collected more than 200 of these stories, originally reported by various missionaries, anthropologists, and ethnologists. While the differences are not always trivial, the common essence of the stories is instructive, as compiled below.

Was there a favored family? 88 percent

Were they forewarned? 66 percent

Was the flood due to the wickedness of man? 66 percent

Was the catastrophe only a flood? 95 percent

Was the flood global? 95 percent

Was survival due to a boat? 70 percent

Did animals play any part? 73 percent

Did survivors land on a mountain? 57 percent

Was the geography local? 82 percent

Were birds sent out? 35 percent

Was the rainbow mentioned? 7 percent

Did survivors offer a sacrifice? 13 percent

Were specifically eight persons saved? 9 percent

Putting the main themes of the accounts together, the story would read something like this:

> Once there was a worldwide flood sent by God to judge the wickedness of man. But there was one righteous family that was forewarned of the coming flood. They built a boat on which they survived the flood along with some animals. As the flood waned, their boat landed on a high mountain, from which they descended and repopulated the whole earth.

Of course, the story sounds much like the biblical story of the great Flood of Noah's day. The most similar accounts are typically from Middle Eastern cultures, but surprisingly similar legends are found in South America, the Pacific islands, and elsewhere. None of these stories contains the beauty, clarity, and believable detail given in the Bible, but each is meaningful to its own culture.

Anthropologists will tell you that a myth is often the faded memory of a real event. Details may have been added, lost, or obscured in the telling and retelling, but the central kernel of truth remains. When two separate cultures have the same story in their body of folklore, their ancestors must have either experienced the same event or they both descended from a common ancestral source that itself experienced the event.

The only credible way to understand the widespread similarity of various flood legends is to recognize that all the people living today have descended from the few people who survived a real global flood on a real boat that eventually landed on a real mountain. Their descendants now fill the globe, never to forget the real event.[2]

Scripture unequivocally teaches that the Flood was global, and does so on many occasions and in many ways. The global Flood interpretation makes good exegetical and logical sense, as well as good theological sense. The Flood narrative is supported by historical evidence, and the next chapter will show that it also has good scientific support.

8

EVIDENCE FROM GEOLOGY

Noah's Flood was unique, and we don't have complete access to everything that happened back then. Today's processes may tell us much, but we can't make firsthand observations. From Scripture we can discern what the Flood was like, and we can look for evidence that supports the account. In particular, we can know that the entire episode was catastrophic and episodic in nature. The pre-Flood world is gone—completely altered. Thus we ought to see evidence in virtually every location. For those who were trained in slow and gradual processes, it comes as a surprise to learn that many leading geologists advocate catastrophism rather than uniformitarianism. It seems that even though many recognize the possibility for catastrophic processes, they fail to take their observations to the rightful conclusion. Many recognize the evidence for megaearthquakes, megatsunamis, and the possibility of extinction-level meteorite impacts and megavolcanoes, near-instantaneous deposition of sediments, rapid erosion, etc. All of these were rejected in the past, but now they are accepted by many. "Put it all together," I tell my secular colleagues. "It's all evidence of a global flood."

These catastrophic processes operated on a global scale. The Bible identifies the Flood as worldwide in scope, but the same processes were not happening at the same time in all places. We would expect to find them acting on a regional, maybe continental scale. Tides in the ocean are influenced by the moon's gravity, and the earth continued to rotate during the Flood, but we don't expect these things to be completely overridden by the Flood's action. Waves are caused primarily by wind; they come in, but then they recede. The Flood was marked by a milieu of geologic and hydraulic events. All the while, the waters continued to come and go until finally all the land was covered. Individual rock layers appear markedly different from other layers of a different source. Marine limestone is quite different from basaltic layers, etc. Geologists easily recognize each geologic layer and can map its extent. All of them, with few exceptions, continue for a regional extent far greater than modern deposits.

Catastrophic deposition operating on a regional extent is perhaps the main signature of the great Flood of Noah's day.

These processes caused a time of unthinkable geological upheaval, such that "the world that then existed perished, being flooded with water" (2 Peter 3:6). No flood in human history has rivaled its destructive magnitude.

Though we are far from a full understanding of the Flood, the Bible does give us a clue when it says, "On that day all the fountains of the great deep were broken up, and the windows of heaven were opened. And the rain was on the earth forty days and forty nights" (Genesis 7:11-12).

The trigger for the Flood was that "all the fountains of the great deep" were ruptured. The fountains may have been underground sources spewing out water and lava into the ocean basins. Evidently there were great subterranean chambers of water that belched forth their contents, causing volcanism and tectonism on a broad scale. After being emptied, some collapsed to become deep sedimentary basins that later uplifted to form mountain chains.

Today when a volcano erupts under water, or if there is an underwater earthquake or mud slide, it causes a tsunami or tidal wave, a dynamic energy wave that pushes water toward the continents and devastates coastal areas. At the start of the Flood, *all* the fountains of the great deep were rent open, sending repeated pulses of water toward the continents from every direction and bringing sediments and marine fossils to the land. Cyclic ocean currents and tidal actions would have left their imprint on these sediments.

Along the mid-ocean ridges, once-molten rock and other superhot fluids would have encountered the ocean, evaporating huge volumes of sea water and ultimately yielding intense rainfall and precipitating their dissolved solids.

Torrential rains poured down. This was a special rain for 40 days and 40 nights, but the deluge continued for 150 days, through the first half of the Flood. This continually replenished source of water would have bombarded the earth, eroding and redepositing sediments on a global scale.

For the next six months, the waters "prevailed" (7:18) upon the earth, with water driven back and forth on the world oceans. Tides were unchecked by shorelines, and until the fountains were stopped and the floodgates closed (8:2-3), any unhardened deposit would be susceptible to reworking in a high-energy environment.

Finally, six months after the start of the Flood, the waters "receded continually from the earth" (8:3). They "decreased continually" for the next several months until the tops of the mountains were seen (verse 5), exposing and drying the land and making it fit for life. This implies continental uplift, the sinking of ocean basins, and the spreading of sea floors. This redistribution of the topography implies extensive deformation of soft, freshly deposited sediments. A great wind aided this drainage (8:1).

The Flood was unmatched by any event in our experience, yet both Scripture and science demands it. Any attempt to reconstruct Earth history that ignores the Genesis Flood is certain to be in gross error.[3]

Some might think that Earth doesn't have that much water, but it does. The Bible even tells us the source of that water. In Genesis 7:11-12, we're told that on one particular day "all the fountains of the great deep were broken up, and the windows of heaven were opened. And the rain was on the earth forty days and forty nights." During creation, God caused some water to remain inside the uplifted continents under great pressure. During the Flood's onset, He allowed the pressurized water to be released and spray upward for 150 days. This caused vast amounts of water contained in the atmosphere to condense and fall as rain. There were 40 days of rain, but the "windows" above were kept open for 150 days, until the windows and the fountains were shut (Genesis 8:2-3), thus ending the Flood.

At the Flood's end, the waters receded. Consider a modern-day photograph of the earth. Most likely you are familiar with the beautiful blue hue that surrounds the globe. This is because water and clouds cover most of the earth. If the photo shows North and South America on the left side, the Atlantic Ocean will be to the right, and as you gaze eastward, you encounter Europe and Africa. Soon you identify Russia and Asia. But a photograph that looks to the west of North and South America will show only water for a long stretch. No land can be seen. About 71 percent of the earth's surface is covered with water. Scripture implies that the continents were prepared to support life, and Genesis teaches that the original continents were uplifted out of water during the creation week for humans and the animals to live upon. The variable elevations of the earth's surface allow the continents to be above water level and the oceans to be quite deep. If the entire planet were smooth—with no mountains and deep oceans—then the earth's surface would be covered by about 10,000 feet of water. So Earth has plenty of water for a global flood. That leads some people to ask, "Where did the water go after the Flood receded?" It's still here—in the oceans!

All the geologic processes that occurred during the Flood and the catastrophic amount of water that washed over the earth formed most of the fossils we see today. Animals are rarely fossilized when they die. Special circumstances are needed for fossilization to occur. When you see a dead dog along the highway, chances are high it will never fossilize. If the carcass remains out in the open, scavengers or bacteria will quickly consume it and oxygen will causes it to decay. Within weeks, all traces of this once-living animal will be gone.

For an animal to become fossilized, it must be buried deeply enough that scavengers and bacteria cannot reach it and oxygen cannot cause it to decay. Yet in spite of the abundance of fossils from the past, this hardly ever happens today. Fossils are found today by the trillions—fossils of every kind and size and shape—but few organisms today are ever fossilized. Most of the fossils we find are marine invertebrates, nearly identical to those living today. Coal is fossilized wood, yet wood is never preserved. Obviously something happened in the past that made it possible for so many animals to perish and be preserved. The Flood, as described in Genesis, fits the bill.

As the water raised and lowered the continents, it also moved them about. This would cause great cracks in the earth, allowing the pressurized water underground to be released. These might have been the "fountains of the great deep" described in Genesis. This spray and volcanic eruptions would have caused the water trapped by the "windows of heaven" to fall to Earth, first in a special downpour of 40 days, then with a torrential downpour for six months. Scientists call the continental movement *plate tectonics*, which progressed rapidly at the time, leaving the earth essentially as we know it today.

In these ways the pre-Flood earth was forever altered. We can only partially reconstruct the old land-mass configurations from what is available today. The modern-day continents are significantly different, having fully "perished," as Scripture teaches (2 Peter 3:6). So we can never find where Noah built the Ark or where the Garden of Eden was located. That world is gone. It was destroyed by the great Flood of Noah's day and was replaced by the modern world—which will eventually undergo another devastating judgment not by water, but by fire.

9

COMMON QUESTIONS

In any discussion about the fact that the Flood was global in nature, many questions arise. This chapter answers some of the more common ones.

Was the Ark big enough to hold all the animals?

During the creation week, God created animals "according to their kind" (Genesis 1:21; see also verses 24-25). We aren't able to study all the animals of the past today, but with regard to those we can study, consider dogs. We know that all dog breeds can interbreed. All varieties came from wolves that were captured, domesticated, and bred. Today we identify dogs by appearance and call them separate breeds, but they are all members of the dog "kind." This includes different species like wolves, coyotes, and domestic dogs. The same could be said of the different cats and horses and frogs. Biblical scientists have calculated that only a few thousand animal kinds were necessary on the Ark to represent the animal kingdom.

Thus, Noah didn't take every *species* of animal, only every *kind*—specifically, he took air-breathing, land-dwelling animals, "all in whose nostrils was the breath of the spirit of life, all that was on the dry land" (Genesis 7:22). The purpose of the Ark was to survive the great Flood, and so Noah certainly didn't have to take fish. Nor did he need to take whales, lobsters, or clams. This would lower the number of animals he had to transport. Only a surprisingly few animal kinds live on land. Certainly marine creatures died by the trillions during the Flood, and we find their fossils today, but some of each marine kind survived and continued to propagate afterward.

The Ark was surprisingly large. The Bible gives its dimensions in *cubits*, and one cubit is approximately 18 inches. The Ark was on the order of 450 feet long, 75 feet wide, and 45 feet high. Seldom was a ship of that size built until modern engineering and steel were available, but the Ark was truly huge. A life-size replica is on exhibit in Kentucky, and its size takes your breath away. Many visitors comment that they had no idea the Ark was so large. Also, the average size of land animals is smaller than a house cat, so the Ark was certainly big enough to carry all the kinds of animals Noah needed to preserve.

It might be appropriate at this point to address extinct animals of great size, like dinosaurs. They lived before the Flood and were probably represented on the Ark. Careful study indicates that they were not as numerous or large as commonly thought. The largest dinosaur fossils are immediately put into museums, but most adult dinosaurs were rather small compared to these giants. Dinosaurs were apparently reptiles, or at least reptile-like. On the pre-Flood earth, even mammals enjoyed long lives, and reptiles typically outlive similar-size mammals. All of them started out as babies, mostly as eggs, and grew throughout their lives. Some grew to colossal sizes!

But the Ark was intended to aid *kinds* of animals through the Flood. The biggest and oldest dinosaurs were not necessarily present. An average adult dinosaur was probably no bigger than a bison. I and others have estimated that many names assigned to dinosaurs could be grouped together into no more than several dozen different kinds. There was plenty of room on the vessel for a few bison-size animals.

How did Noah and his family collect all the animals?

Interestingly enough, Noah was never told by God to go and collect the animals needed for preservation. Instead, he was only told to build the Ark, and once he was finished and the time was right, God caused the animals to come to him. Standard thinking holds the idea that the world has always been similar to our present-day world, with animals living scattered around the globe, adapted to various habitats. Not so in Scripture. There we find the entire pre-Flood world of moderate temperature and without barriers like oceans or mountain ranges. Animals of all types evidently lived comfortably around the globe. We can suspect that they were able to migrate when necessary. "And they went into the ark to Noah, two by two, of all flesh in which is the breath of life...and the LORD shut him in" (Genesis 7:15-16). Animal behaviorists have noticed that land animals tend to migrate just before disaster strikes.

How could they care for the animals once on board?

Authorities have noticed that when animals are confined under great stress, they have a tendency to go into a state of minimal energy and activity. This is much like hibernation. They require less food, exercise, and care. While Noah and his family still needed to tend to the animals, the requirements probably weren't as demanding as we might think.

I am not hypothesizing that all the animals marched in an orderly line into the Ark, or that once loaded they hibernated, and when the Ark was opened again, they immediately migrated away afterward. But these traits do exist in most animals today. They were not needed before the Flood, and authorities have little explanation for the origin of these marvelous traits. But such characteristics would have been a sweet gift of God's grace when needed most by Noah and his family.

How did the Ark survive the Flood's turmoil?

The Ark's dimensions are special. God designed the Ark to survive, and Noah built it to His precise specifications. From a normal standpoint, the vessel would have been in great peril during the Flood. Experts have noted that the biggest danger would be a chance broadside by a powerful wave, but the Ark's long length (450 feet or so) would tend to keep it pointed *into* the waves. The cross-section of 45 feet in height by 75 feet in width would cause gravity forces downward and buoyant forces upward, which would help keep the Ark from being capsized. For any degree of tilt up to 90 degrees, the two parallel but opposite forces would force the Ark back upright. Modern-day shipbuilding engineers have tested God's design and deem it the best possible design. God knew what He was doing, and He designed the Ark for the survival of its living cargo.

Is the discovery of the Ark prophesied in Scripture?

The Bible gives much detail regarding the construction, utilization, and ultimate meaning of the Ark, but it has no word at all regarding its preservation following the Flood. No prophecy regarding a discovery can be found. In fact, much of what we think we know about the Ark is derived from inference and from the understanding of God's nature when dealing with man in times of calamity. There's much we do not know.

For instance, the term "mountains of Ararat" on its own is a mystery. *Ararat* was the name of an ancient country, so the term's appearance in Scripture actually tells us that the Ark rested somewhere within this country. But where? While there is a mountain called Mt. Ararat, this same mountain has different names in other languages. In Turkish it is *Agri Dagi*, or "Painful Mountain." In Armenian it goes by *Masis*. Europeans adopted the name *Ararat*, and it stuck. Having said that, those living on the mountain throughout history have always accepted the idea that this was the place Noah's journey ended. Many names of nearby places reflect this tradition. And nearly all the eyewitnesses who claim to have seen the Ark—hundreds of them—place it on this mountain. Because there is no strong tradition that it was seen elsewhere, we feel justified in looking for it on Mt. Ararat.

How could only Noah and his family build the Ark?

From Scripture you get the impression that Noah built the Ark alone with the help of his three grown sons. We are told the ages of the family members only, but they could have been wealthy enough to hire other workers. We are not told of woodworking experience, but we get the impression that Noah was told 120 years beforehand that the Flood judgment was coming and to get ready (Genesis 6:3). How efficiently could four men do the job? All we know is that after a few years, they were experienced workers. Good workers today can fell trees, transport them to the job site, plane the lumber, and assemble it in a rather short time. So we conclude the job could have been accomplished within the time frame God gave to Naoh. The Ark was not necessarily a finished show-piece, but it was seaworthy enough to float and keep its occupants safe.

Why did God give the sign of the rainbow?

Noah and his family had just come through an unimaginably fright-ening experience. It's possible they had never even seen a storm, and cer-tainly not one like this. It would remain constant in their memories for years to come. During the Flood, the winds howled incessantly and the thunder pealed continually as the Ark pitched and rolled in the waves. Earthquakes rocked the planet without stop, sending pulsating tsunamis in every direction. Underwater volcanoes and the spreading "fountains of the great deep" (Genesis 7:11) heated the water surrounding the Ark, making life on board almost unbearable. Continuous rainfall pelted the Ark's roof, as if it were passing under Niagara Falls.

This was not merely a Category 5 hurricane. Creationists speculate about *hypercanes*—storms dozens of times greater than present-day hur-ricanes. Surely the pre-Flood world fully "perished" (2 Peter 3:6) under such an onslaught.

As Noah and his family stepped off the Ark, they entered a world totally unfamiliar to them. The geography had all changed. Plant and ani-mal life had been devastated. Weather patterns were chaotic. Gone was the pre-Flood stability they were accustomed to. Contrast that to the rel-ative stability we enjoy today.

It would perhaps have taken several centuries for Earth to settle down to the present pseudo-equilibrium. After all, the jet streams would have needed time to stabilize. The ocean currents had to find their "paths of the seas" (Psalm 8:8). The continents had to halt their rapid horizontal movements and cease their vertical uplift. In particular, the oceans would have needed time to give up their excess heat, which would have caused further violent storm patterns.

It was into this unstable world Noah and his family disembarked. No doubt earthquakes were common. Of necessity they lived in tents because it was not possible to make structures that would have withstood the earthquakes. Wood was in short supply, and rock structures were the least safe.

Rainfall continued with swollen streams and violent storms. Calculations show that the ocean's heat would have taken at least 600 years or so to dissipate, and that during this period the Ice Age dominated. Job lived soon after the Flood, and his book contains more references to ice and snow than the rest of the Bible put together. Up until perhaps the time of Abraham, the world was quite a dangerous place on account of many natural catastrophes.

No doubt Noah's family needed reassurance that there would never be another Flood like the one they had just experienced. Thus, it was out of God's grace and mercy that He instituted this beautiful reminder of His protection. And every time they saw a rainbow, it would serve as a majestic reminder of the security they have in Him.[4]

10
THE SEARCH GOES ON

My personal efforts toward finding the Ark are over. Through the years, some of my friends have taken up the search and extended it even more. Some have taken it to different locations. Many notice that, in the Koran, the Ark came to rest on Mount Cudi (sounds like *Judy* because *c* in Turkish is pronounced *j*), which is located in southern Turkey and is not very tall. It seems unlikely that the Ark would have landed there, but it is within the mountains of Ararat and warrants our attention.

More convincing research has been undertaken by Dr. Randall Price, a professional archaeologist on the faculty at Liberty University. For the past several years, he has launched a well-funded and well-planned effort based on satellite imagery to uncover something potentially beneath the glacier near the 17,000-foot summit. The grueling and dangerous efforts to excavate through hundreds of feet of ice have not resulted in their expected goal. He leaves the expedition door ajar, but efforts to discover the elusive Ark remain unfruitful. We are waiting for others—perhaps even readers of this booklet—to continue the search.

The truth of the great Flood of Noah's day can never be forgotten. We encounter the evidence everywhere we go. We come across it every time we study or even see nature. We are forced to ponder the ways of God when we look at the remains of the Flood, like rocks and fossils. He has revealed the truth of creation and the Flood, complete with news of His holy nature. God hates sin—always has and always will. He has declared the ultimate penalty for sin to be death. And He is not the sort of God to let sin go unpunished. We know that we are sinners who have broken His law and are under His righteous death penalty.

We can do nothing to alter this fact any more than someone in Noah's day who, by disbelieving Noah's proclamation that the great Flood was coming, could have stopped it from coming. The Flood came anyway, just as God's judgment is coming. In fact, Jesus Christ Himself compared the coming judgment by fire to the past judgment by water (Matthew 24:37-39). No one will escape.

But just as in Noah's day, He provides a way of escape to those who believe. Noah and his family were saved. Everyone else perished. In our case, God has provided His only Son, our Lord and Savior Jesus Christ. He came to Earth as a sinless man who had no death penalty of His own to pay. By so doing, He was qualified to die for you and me. He died as a sacrifice so that we wouldn't have to die. We must simply believe that He died in our place, offering us forgiveness of our sins. And that He rose from the grave, having conquered death, offering us eternal life.

The Ark account is then of ultimate importance to us. Just as the believers in that day had to board the Ark for safety, so we must accept God's free gift of forgiveness and eternal life through the work of Jesus Christ on the cross by believing that it applies to us.

Settle it forever with Him. Come to Him in faith, and He will respond with forgiveness, adoption into His family, and eternal life.

It may be that as a symbol of that salvation, the Ark still rests somewhere on Mt. Ararat. Many expeditions over the years, including mine, have attempted to find it, but none so far have been definitively successful. Perhaps God will never allow the Ark to be found. We may never know. Until then, the search continues for the last remaining link to the "world that then existed" (2 Peter 3:6).

APPENDIX A
APPLICATION LETTER FOR THE
1972 EXPEDITION TO MT. ARARAT

In the months preceding the Institute for Creation Research's expedition to Mt. Ararat in 1972, many qualified and concerned individuals contacted me and asked to be included in the search. I and others prayed diligently over each applicant and wrote a short letter or called to inform these men that the Lord did not seem to indicate that they were the right ones for the job. But there were three men to whom I wrote the following letter. These three men had the right qualifications, and the more we prayed about them, the clearer it became that these were the men whom God had chosen to continue the search for the remains of Noah's Ark.

Dear _____,

Thank you for your letter indicating your interest in joining our Ararat expedition. We are still in need of men to join us in the search, but have made it a matter of real prayer that the Lord make known His will to us and that the right group of men will be drawn together.

Before any decision is made concerning your personal involvement,

I would like to acquaint you with our specific plans and also the dangers involved. If, after reading this letter and seeking God's will, you still feel led to join us, contact me or my second-in-command, John Seiter, at this same address.

To begin with, each member of the team will be required to undergo a week of intensive training on Mt. Hood, near Portland, Oregon, to master the techniques of glacial travel, rescue, and survival. This training is scheduled for the middle of June.

While I have no doubt that you are physically fit and can successfully climb Mt. Ararat, I want to make sure that you realize the dangers and hardships involved. For the most part, we will be on or just below a glacier, the permanent ice cap of the mountain. Problems with crevasses, landslides, rockslides, and blizzards will be everyday occurrences. When not on the glacier itself, we will be traveling through and sleeping in the territory of the Kurds. The Kurds live on the slopes of the mountain and are subject to no formal legal system. Some of them are also capable of slitting one's throat as he sleeps. The Turkish Army, which patrols the area, will not allow us to continue the search if we are suspected of any anti-Turkish activities, since Mt. Ararat is near the border of Turkey and Russia. Some people have been shot instantly in such situations, and others arrested for spying.

My point is this—this endeavor should not be confused with a romantic adventure. There is a real possibility of injury and even death. In fact, the obstacles are so numerous that a successful search would be impossible without the help of God.

Concerning finances, each member of the team is responsible for paying his own way. No general appeal for money has been made, simply because we want to remain inconspicuous. Several people have donated money throughout the past few months, and it will be used for needs that concern the entire group. The personal cost for each person will be $2,000.

Dedication to the task of finding the Ark is a prime requirement and is an overriding issue in the selection of personnel. Of the five-man team, only three will be together on the upper reaches of the mountain at any time. These three, however, will have to climb the treacherous slopes with up to a 75-pound pack on their backs, endure extreme weather conditions, eat lukewarm dehydrated food, and sleep in a crawl-in tent for a week at a time. Each member must be willing to take orders and submit to the leader's direction. There will be no room for arguments, bickering, and insubordination.

Upon returning to the States, it is hoped that we will have the chance to share our experiences with interested churches and schools. Our purpose in finding the Ark is not to gain wealth or fame but to win souls for Jesus Christ, and our hope is that the evidence we bring back will cause many people to believe God's Word. It is likely that many churches and Christian groups will desire speakers who were directly involved with the discovery of the Ark to come and share their experiences and findings with them. We have an obligation to God to use this opportunity to further His kingdom here on Earth. If this is not your goal and desire as a Christian, then you should not consider joining our group.

Let me summarize the requirements for prospective personnel in order of their importance, as I see them:

1. Theology—Be sound in conservative Christian doctrine and have a deep desire to see people come to know Jesus Christ as their Lord and Savior.

2. Dedication—Have a willingness to risk life and health to find Noah's Ark because of its evangelical implications.

3. Personality—Have a personality that is harmonious with the others in the group and a determination to maintain goodwill and peace.

4. Speaking Ability—Possess the means and desire to tell others of the meaning of Noah's Ark.

5. Physical Ability—Have the physical strength and endurance needed to climb one of the highest mountains in the world.

6. Financial Backing—The ability to pay one's own way or to raise the support without any commitments to non-Christian organizations.

I have tried to portray to you in this letter just what to expect in regard to our trip. I have been as honest and straightforward as possible. I want to make sure that you know what is involved before you reaffirm your desire to join our group. I think you should talk it over with your family and diligently seek God's will before making a decision.

Please write me and tell me more about yourself, your religious background and Christian life, your personal dedication to this cause, and your thoughts about the trip. We have prayed daily that the Lord will provide the right men for the job, and if He has spoken to you in this matter, please let me know.

Yours for the Ark,
John D. Morris

APPENDIX B
ARK UPDATES

Dr. John Morris wrote these three articles during the years he searched for the Ark.

The Search for Noah's Ark: 1983[5]

During late August and early September 1983, a small group of explorers sponsored by and representing ICR was allowed to climb Mt. Ararat in search of Noah's Ark. The climbing team concentrated its efforts on the west and north sides of the mountain, particularly the east side of the Ahora Gorge, thought to be the most likely site for the remains of the Ark.

The writer was once again the leader of the expedition, having directed the project since the early 1970s. We returned to the mountain on August 19 with a scaled-down crew of four Americans and one Turkish resident of America. Three of the team were mountaineering experts, two of whom were also trained in mountain rescue and medicine. One of these mountaineers, Donald Barber of San Diego, re-activated a previous injury at the 9,500-ft. level and was unable to continue the climb. The other mountaineers, ex-medic Brian Bartlett of Samuels, Idaho, and Dr. Ahmet Arslan of Washington, DC, an expert on Turkish folklore, native of Mt. Ararat, as well as professional climber, did make the climb. They were joined by Ed Crawford of Edmonton, Alberta, trained in Sumerian culture and cuneiform, and the writer. These were accompanied on the mountain by Ahmet Shaheen, vice-president of the Turkish Alpine Federation, and two Kurdish residents of Mt. Ararat. A return date of

September 7 was necessary because of prior commitments, the group having planned to begin the work earlier in the summer.

The permits which had been requested beginning in early July were delayed until a very complete screening and evaluation process was completed by the Turkish government. In contrast to nearly all past expeditions, ICR applied for and was granted full scientific research permits by the Turkish government. The group proposed to study archaeological remains in the Ararat area, make linguistic and cultural comparisons with remains at sites known to be of great antiquity, and to test the ICR position that all civilizations had originally sprung from a common source: the survivors of the Flood who lived on Mt. Ararat. Specific plans had originally included careful documentation and evaluation of known inscriptions, relief drawings, underground chambers, and structures previously discovered in the vicinity of Mt. Ararat, while also searching the area for other ancient relics, including the remains of the Ark. All members of the ICR team were specialists chosen specifically as men capable of accomplishing these goals.

Although the permits were finally granted and research visas issued by the Turkish embassy in Washington, DC, finalization of the necessary paperwork kept the ICR group off the mountain for still another week and a half of precious time. While waiting, they revisited an unexcavated cave in the foothills of Ararat which has been known but never publicized to any extent until John Morris's books in 1973 and 1975.[6,7] The cave, which had been dated as pre-Hittite based on the carvings and inscriptions near its opening, is hand-carved into an upturned layer of sandy limestone. Many more aspects of this site were discovered, including a series of prepared ledges and a facade which had been smoothed off near the cave opening in preparation for additional inscriptions or openings. Unfortunately, much deterioration of the area has taken place since 1975 and an interior room (tomb area?) as well as an arched tunnel had collapsed. The excavation of this promising site remains of paramount importance in the understanding of the early civilizations which sprang up after the Flood.

The other important archaeological site which ICR had hoped to document was declared a restricted zone and access was impossible. Objects discovered on past expeditions include a large semicircular altar, a cave with eight Sumerian crosses on its entry, inscriptions in a precuneiform script, and many other objects of obvious antiquity. Much fruitful work could be done at this site.

Instead of beginning their climb on the northern side, which lies within the sensitive zone adjacent to the Russian border as they had hoped, the ICR team was forced to climb from the south side on the standard tourist route to the summit and then to traverse around to the west and north. Implications of this ruling included losing four days of the limited remaining time in ascent and descent, inability to establish a base camp with proper documentary and climbing gear, and many miles of dangerous climbing on loose glacial skree.

Once at the Ahora Gorge, however, the team did check out what were thought to be the most promising sites from vantage points above as well as below. No wood of any sort was discovered. Two new inscriptions were discovered on loose rocks in the bottom of the Ahora Gorge made of a stone common on the west face of the gorge. Another hand-carved cave which is easily seen on the vertical west wall of the gorge is reported to contain objects of religious significance by Kurdish villagers, none of whom have ventured there for superstitious reasons. Indeed, it would be nearly impossible to do so without technical rock climbing skills and equipment. Due to the reduced quantity and type of technical equipment brought on the long climb from the starting point on the south side of the mountain, the ICR team was disappointed in its efforts to enter the cave. Climbing from below was unsafe due to loose rock. A two-rope-length rappel down from above stopped about 10 meters above the cave.[8]

Those knowledgeable on the Ararat project know that late August is considered the optimum time to search. The weather becomes much more unpredictable and potentially violent in September and climbing may become quite dangerous. Reports of a record winter snowfall had dampened expectations for the summer's work, as did news reports of bad weather in mid-August. But the ICR team found the mountain rather hospitable for a change, although cloud cover hampered photography and two midday snowstorms forced temporary bivouacs. Each day the snow melted and very little snow remained below 14,000-ft. elevation, while the glaciers had receded back farther than in anyone's memory. The conditions seemed optimum for a discovery.

Other aspects of danger were also avoided. Relationships with the local Kurds on the mountain were enhanced by participation of the two Turkish guides and the assistance of two well-respected Kurdish villagers. Thankfully, only a few minor skirmishes occurred with the usually vicious Kurdish wolfhounds. Furthermore, even though the team spent many hours and traveled many miles over loose "crumbly rock," only rare avalanches caused concern, with no injuries. We did encounter a bear in an ice cave on a hot afternoon in the Ahora Gorge, but thankfully he was not interested in us.

Despite the favorable conditions, no remains of the Ark were discovered. Those sites thought to be the most likely resting places for the Ark were thoroughly investigated and photographed. Other sites of less interest could have been checked out, but time was short. (As it was, the writer had to miss the first three weeks of his teaching duties for the fall semester and could not stay longer.) The team returned to the States on September 8 and 10, satisfied that they had done everything possible under the circumstances. They and their financial and prayer supporters were predictably disappointed that the Ark was not discovered but rest in the fact that God will allow the discovery in His time, and not before.

Turkey has recently changed its long-standing position against research and travel in the Ararat area. Whereas for the last 10 years or so access has been quite limited, many groups from countries around the world were allowed to climb to the summit this year. Several expeditions were not restricted to the standard summit route and were allowed to look elsewhere in search of Noah's Ark.

One such expedition consisted of Pat Frost, Dr. Howard Davis, Dr. James Davies, and others who linked up with a Turkish group doing medical research on the mountain. They achieved good coverage of the North Canyon area and the area west of the Ahora Gorge. Another, headed up by Dr. John Willis, excavated a portion of an interesting ice pack east of the summit at 16,000-ft. elevation with a modified chainsaw adapted to ice. Still another group, John McIntosh and friends, spent some time searching the area east of the Gorge and toward the saddle between the two peaks. They then joined still another group headed by former astronaut Colonel James Irwin and including Eryl Cummings, Marvin Steffins, Ray Anderson, and climber Bob Stuplich. This latter expedition was even allowed to make plane trips around the mountain. Unfortunately, their photos showed no objects of interest. Neither did their ground search, which explored the east side of the Ahora Gorge and toward the saddle. A final group intended to make a late-season attempt as the ICR group left the mountain, and as of this writing have not returned.

The obvious thought has now crossed each explorer's mind—perhaps the remains of the Ark are not really on the mountain at all. Yet the overwhelming evidence remains.[9] Something must be up there. But where? Seemingly, every possible location has been checked. On the other hand, it may be that our methods are no longer productive. Since none of these difficult and expensive foreign expeditions have been fruitful, in part due to their inability to spend large amounts of time on the mountain, perhaps it is time to turn the search over to the actual inhabitants, who have ready access to the mountain.

Just such a solution has been proposed and is being carefully considered. An ICR supporter has recently pledged a substantial sum of money to be offered as a reward to any Turkish discoverer of the Ark. The money would be placed in a Turkish bank and would be released once an ICR observer has documented the discovery. Until the Ark is found, no money would be spent and no lives endangered. If accepted, the offer will be extended to the proper Turkish groups within the next few months.

Those who might question such a plan should bear in mind that the combined expenditures of just this one summer's various expeditions totaled well over a quarter of a million dollars. A reward may well be a better use of limited finances and seems now to offer a greater chance for success. Readers of *Acts & Facts* will be kept apprised of events as they occur.

A Report on the ICR Ararat Expedition, 1987[10]

It has been obvious for some time that ground-based expeditions to Mt. Ararat in search of Noah's Ark have very little chance of succeeding. All who have seen pictures of the mountain and heard of the difficulties and dangers fully understand the necessity of using other methods.

This past August, the Institute for Creation Research (ICR) partici-pated in an international expedition comprised of representatives of four organizations in cooperation with two Turkish companies. This consor-tium was granted permission by the currently very cooperative central government in Ankara (1) to survey and photograph all areas of inter-est on the mountain from a fixed-wing airplane, (2) to investigate with a high-altitude helicopter any promising sites discovered from the aircraft or aerial photos, and (3) to document any discovery by a ground-based climbing party. As a requirement of this permit, we were asked to do an equivalent study of the boat-shaped formation some 20 miles away from Ararat, which others have suspected might be the decayed remains of Noah's Ark. (I have studied this formation and am convinced it is merely an unusual geologic formation.)

Although all involved organizations participated in planning at all stages, primary responsibility for the acquisition and interpretation of aerial photographs lay with ICR and International Exploration, Inc. (Interex, Mr. Rod Keller, president), a Canadian-based aerial exploration company. A Cessna 206 aircraft was leased from a Turkish aircraft dealer in Ankara, capable of flying to 20,000-feet elevation and equipped with a high-resolution camera. The request to use a sensitive infrared video cam-era was withdrawn during permit negotiations.

High Flight Foundation of Colorado Springs (former astronaut Jim Irwin, director) accepted primary responsibility for the use of the helicopter—a Jet Ranger II with pre-engine, also leased from a Turkish company, as well as direction of potential ground exploration and docu-mentation. Plans to use the helicopter to build a mountaineering shelter at the request of the Turkish Mountaineering Federation were cancelled since the final permissions were not granted until mid-August—much too late for transportation and construction.

Evangelische Omroep (EO), a branch of official government televi-sion in the Netherlands (Jon Van Den Boesch, director), under separate permits to film in Turkey, was joined to the Ararat expedition to docu-ment all activities and discoveries. EO has had a long and fruitful involve-ment in creationist activities, including the original filming of the movies now known as the award-winning series *Origins: How the World Came to Be.*

As is always the case, difficulties and opposition surfaced at every turn. Our permit received approval on August 14, but getting the specific aspects nailed down and paperwork completed turned out to be a trying process (as it would also be in any country). By August 25, however, we had explicit documents allowing all phases of our work, including the basing of both helicopter and airplane in Doğubeyazit, the town at the base of the mountain. Precise flight plans had been approved by the Civil Aviation Agency, and although cautious, our hopes were high.

Earlier in the spring, however, a directive had been issued from the prime minister (not normally involved in the permit process) mandating that no exploration of any sort would be allowed on Mt. Ararat, evidently in response to requests from certain American groups interested in promoting the boat-shaped formation as the Ark. Even though the evidence favoring this site is quite meager and speculative, there is a government effort to capitalize on the attention given it, including the building of a "visitor's center" on the site and improvement of the road to it. I had learned of this directive but assumed our permission constituted an exception to it.

Unfortunately, therefore, provincial and local officials with responsibility to implement our permits had two conflicting documents, and clarification and coordination turned out to be impossible. At 10:00 p.m. on the night before we were to begin flying, we were told by the local officials that the more restrictive of the two was to be honored, and the flights were cancelled.

A second major problem dealt with the nearness of both Russian and Iranian borders. By agreement with these countries, Turkey maintains a 20-km buffer zone along these borders, within which activities such as our proposed exploration and photography are kept to a minimum. However, our permits specifically allowed us to land in Doğubeyazit (about 10 km from Iran), and specifically approved the areas of research on the mountain (slightly over 20 km from Russia, but only about 15 km from Iran). Again, local officials had two conflicting orders, and chose the more restrictive.

A third problem merits mention. The winter of 1987 had seen record amounts of snowfall in Eastern Turkey, and since the snow covering might obscure anything on the ground, this was thought to be detrimental to the search. Conversely, the summer had produced record heat waves, and all Ararat veterans felt the snow meltback was at least better than average. More importantly, the night on which our permits were cancelled, a major snowstorm hit the mountain, leaving at least 18 inches of new snow, covering everything above 11,000 feet elevation. This had melted within a week, but by then our permits had been revoked.

After extensive negotiation, we were finally allowed to make one flight, of course restricted to air space outside the 20-km buffer zones. This meant we could photograph the west side of the mountain and see the promising north side only obliquely, from high altitude. Unfortunately, low-lying clouds covered the mountain below 13,000 feet, and the recent snowfall obscured much of what remained.

The photographs taken, however, are of excellent quality, and do provide insight into a few areas of interest. They were taken in such a way as to provide stereoscopic coverage of the areas photographed, allowing three-dimensional viewing. The photos have now been carefully studied, and sadly, no hints of the Ark have been seen.

We are now involved in ongoing discussions with officials of the Turkish government and private parties, including an attempt to understand fully the scenario that kept us from realizing our research goals this past summer, and inquiries into the best way to proceed from here. We are even now exploring a way to achieve these same goals with minimal involvement from non-Turks, among other things.

Even though we didn't do all we had hoped to do, in the final analysis, we were able to secure governmental permission for an aerial search—an answer to a 16-year prayer of mine. We are now much more aware of the implementation process and of Turkish law bearing on this issue, and know the ways to eliminate the specific problems which stymied us. Now is hardly the time to quit! The mechanism is in place and relationships established which might yield a proper survey next August.

Also, EO filmed extensive interviews with me on the foothills of Mt. Ararat, discussing the nature of the Flood and the search for the Ark. Questions like, "Where did the water of the Flood come from?" "Where did it go?" "How could Noah get all the animals on board the Ark?"

"How could he care for the animals?" etc. were answered. It is hoped that these interviews will result in a popular teaching video in the months ahead.

Meanwhile, efforts are continuing to evaluate recent high-resolution satellite imagery of Mt. Ararat. Computer enhancement technique, developed for the data from the French SPOT satellite, makes it possible to identify objects as little as three meters in diameter. ICR is committed to this study and involved in two such efforts.

As you may know, scores of individuals and groups applied for Ararat permits this past summer. In many Turkish government offices, the whole search has become a joke. Many of the applicants have no credibility, no experience, no workable plan, have done no preparation, and seemingly have no reasonable chance for success. Many claim divine guidance and knowledge of the whereabouts of the Ark. Nearly all, having no understanding of nor regard for Turkish customs, regularly offend all they meet. Thankfully, our scientific and well-structured effort has been recognized by most officials, but the ill will created by other groups spills over. The point is this: Since all groups raise money from Christians, I would encourage you to investigate and invest your money carefully.

The evidence continues to mount that the Lord has protected the Ark over the years since the Flood. In spite of the volcanic eruptions, the earthquakes, the erosion of the glacier, and the effects of time, the data strongly assert that the remains of the Ark lie somewhere on Mt. Ararat, buried by volcanic debris and ice, awaiting the proper time. God answers prayer, and we can be thankful for the progress made this summer. In *His* time and to *His* glory, the obstacles will be overcome and the Ark will be found. Even though the disappointment of this last summer is still fresh, I am convinced the discovery is near.

The Search for Noah's Ark: Status 1992[11]

Since the search for the Ark began in the 1940s, evidence has continued to mount that the remains of a barge-like structure still exist somewhere on Mt. Ararat in eastern Turkey. This evidence consists primarily of reports by individuals who claim to have seen the Ark. Unfortunately, none of these accounts have been substantiated by documentation. Thus, all are to some degree questionable, and each should be held lightly. It can rightly be said that without these "eyewitness" reports, there would be no reason to look for the Ark, for the Bible contains no prophecy that it would be found. Indeed, it would be unlikely to have survived, apart from providential intervention.

These "eyewitnesses" all describe the Ark in the same general fashion—a large rectangular barge, usually with a catwalk, a "window" running its entire length. They likewise describe it as being high on the mountain, but not as high as the summit. They generally claim that only a portion of it can be seen, usually at the end of a long, hot summer, the rest covered by snow or rock. Most claim it is in very steep terrain, perhaps on a ledge adjacent to a cliff. For a variety of reasons, no one has been able to pinpoint the location.

The Bible claims that "the Ark came to rest on the mountains of Ararat" (Genesis 8:4 NIV). Ararat was a region—a country—in the time of Moses, which included the mountain today known as Mt. Ararat, and much other territory. Thus the Bible does not specify a location in this region other than implying a high elevation, for it took two-and-one-half months for other mountains to appear (verse 5). The main reason to look on greater Mt. Ararat is because the majority of the eyewitnesses identify it as the site of their discovery, and their stories, which are unrelated, substantially agree.

The Bible tells us something of the construction of the Ark (Genesis 6:14-16) with three stories, a "window" structure on top, and "pitch" within and without. Noah was commanded to build it with "rooms" for the animals.

The "gopher wood," from which the Ark was made, is unidentified, and some have even speculated that it may have been a synthetic material.

The gross dimensions are given in cubits: three hundred cubits long by fifty cubits wide and thirty cubits high. A cubit is usually thought to be the distance from a man's elbow to his fingertips, but it seemed to vary from one civilization to another. Estimates vary from 17.5 inches to 24 inches. For convenience, most use a conservative figure of 18 inches, making the Ark 450 feet by 75 feet by 45 feet. Even at that, it was a huge vessel, certainly big enough to carry two (or in some cases seven) of each "kind" of land-dwelling, air-breathing animal. Beyond these few details, nothing more is said of the Ark, other than that it was sufficient for the journey.

My first trip to eastern Turkey was in 1971, and I have returned twelve times since, the last being in 1989. Some expeditions have been more successful than others, but each has been an adventure. The difficulties primarily lie in gaining access to the mountain from the central government and in dealing with local officials. Once on the mountain, we have been able to search a number of specific sites and have discovered many archaeological remains, but the Ark itself has not been found. Several other expeditions have also joined the search, with similar results.

Traditionally, the search was on foot, but in recent years the Turkish government has allowed the use of both helicopters and airplanes. Since ground expeditions usually have been only minimally effective, there is, in my opinion, no reason for further climbing expeditions, except perhaps for sonar surveys on the ice cap itself, and also to check out discoveries made from the air.

Political instability in the area limits access to eastern Turkey. Most notably, the Kurdish minority has been clamoring for independence, a movement which has gained international attention due to the tragic plight of ethnic Kurds in Iraq, not far to the south. The borders of Turkey, Iran, and the former Soviet state, Armenia, all come together at the base of Mt. Ararat, with predictable tensions. The recent breakup of the Soviet Union has further destabilized the area, as Armenia and Azerbaijan feud over borders.

Well-planned expeditions with high-altitude helicopters and sensitive scientific equipment received permission to search from both air and ground in 1990 and 1991, but each was cancelled over the issue of Iraq and Kuwait, and then the Kurdish problem ensued.

On a personal note, with my own responsibilities at ICR increasing over the years, I have found it necessary to cut back on my involvement in the search. My interest remains, but I have no plans to launch another ICR-sponsored expedition. However, I have maintained contact with the various expeditions actively seeking permits, and there remains the possibility that I would consider participating in a well-planned, high-tech, aerial search. Other than that, I maintain sincere friendships with other groups involved but only nominally keep abreast of activities.

Interestingly enough, there are a few individuals who claim the Ark has already been found. They point to an interesting boat-shaped formation discovered in 1959 in a Turkish aerial mapping project. It is situated some twenty miles from the summit of Greater Ararat (i.e., within the "mountains of Ararat"), is of a size compatible with the biblical dimensions (515 feet by 138 feet), and is in a streamlined "boat shape."

The site has been investigated several times over the years, first in 1960 by a joint Turkish-American expedition, then by several groups in the '60s and '70s. My first efforts to study it in 1975 were thwarted by the local military, but two subsequent surveys were more fruitful. My conclusion, and the conclusion of almost every other team, was that it is an unusual geologic phenomenon and not Noah's Ark.

In the late 1970s, Mr. Ron Wyatt began studying the area. While a nonscientist, Wyatt tirelessly surveyed the area, eventually marshaling several lines of evidence to support his contention that this formation is Noah's Ark. Eventually, Wyatt joined forces with David Fasold, Dr. John Baumgardner, Dr. Allen Roberts, and others.

Baumgardner, a geophysicist, was able to perform several scientific tests on the site, [using] magnetometry, ground-penetrating radar, seismic, and finally, core drilling. Although he was at first open to the possibility that the site was the Ark, Baumgardner now contends he has disproved the hypothesis, especially by the core-drilling, which revealed only the sorts of rock on the nearby hillsides, and nothing of archaeological significance.

Meanwhile, Wyatt and Fasold have both published books on the "discovery" of the Ark, although they have now parted company and disagree about many of the important details.

Wyatt claims he has found much petrified wood, of a type which had no tree rings. (He holds that pre-Flood trees had no rings.) Fasold claims the Ark was constructed of cemented reeds which have since decayed away. Wyatt talks of the remains of three decks, rooms, and timbers, while Fasold feels the impression of the decayed ship is about all that remains. Both refer to "drogue stones," or stones suspended by rope from a boat and used to maintain stability and navigation. Both refer to corroded metal fittings, which they claim are found in rows, delineating the "ribs of the ship," as indicated by metal detectors and especially a "molecular frequency generator." This device, called a *molecular frequency generator* by Wyatt, which includes two handheld brass rods that cross when the sub-surface target is located, has been used by both to generate significant aspects of their data. Let me comment briefly on each of these points.

On my two field studies and the investigations by many others, and in the microscopic study of samples gathered at the site, no petrified wood has been found. The rock types are somewhat exotic, but I have found neither wood nor cemented reeds. (By the way, petrified woods from before the Flood do have tree rings. Evidently, while the seasons may not have been as pronounced, they were sufficient to produce rings in the woody trees, as is obvious by studying petrified wood from numerous geologic layers.)

The reliable subsurface tests do show distinct buried layers, but core drilling identified these layers as rock surfaces natural to the area.

The drogue stones are found at some distance from the site, the nearest one, to my knowledge, being fourteen miles away. They are not dissimilar to many tombstones in the area, and are currently found in graveyards.

The metal "fittings" are a serious overstatement. Much metallic ore is present in the surrounding hillsides and on the site. Furthermore, igneous cobbles are frequently present, which contain high concentrations of naturally occurring magnetic minerals. A metal detector will indicate this high concentration, which could be mistaken for a metal object. The sporadic cobbles were not found in a straight line, according to those present at the time, but ribbons connecting the locations of these cobbles did obviously appear in a line. Subsequent metal-detector surveys by several independent parties, including Baumgardner, have not discerned any pattern.

The molecular frequency generator, with its crossing, handheld brass rods appears to employ the ancient art of divination—a practice thoroughly condemned by Scripture. At best, the results are hardly considered trustworthy. But it is this device which has produced the main support for the claim of metal fittings.

Both Fasold and Wyatt are articulate and assertive in their manner, and many have been convinced. They have aggressively promoted themselves and their works, and in so doing have intimidated many and frustrated serious scientists and Ark searchers. Both have shown a tendency to attack, personally, those who disagree with them. In their writings and interviews, each has demonstrated disdain for Christians in general and ICR in particular.

The site itself has received some attention with Turkey, and there is an effort to promote it as the Ark, in hopes of receiving tourist dollars. An unfurnished "visitor's center" has been built overlooking the site. Unfortunately, getting to the site is difficult. A narrow, rutted dirt road winds up a steep hillside to a nearby village, but it is not navigable by many cars. Claims of a six-lane highway leading to the site are false.

My own geologic survey, coupled with microscopic analysis of all the rocks gathered and the thoughts of Baumgardner and others, has led to the conclusion that the formation, which rests between two hills on the side of a larger hillside, was formed as soil and mud slid downhill around a stable area, leaving a streamlined shape. Suffice it to say that there is a perfectly straightforward geologic explanation for the formation and absolutely no indication that it is of archaeological significance.

Efforts to launch meaningful expeditions in the summer of 1992 were minimized by ongoing tensions in the area. But while the search has changed over the years and been tainted with much controversy, there is no shortage of veterans who want to return, and new groups attempting to launch their own efforts. We trust any future expedition will be conducted with integrity, all the while bathed in prayer, for until God intervenes, the Ark's whereabouts will remain a mystery.

APPENDIX C
GENESIS SPECIFIES THE FLOOD WAS GLOBAL

Genesis 6 (NKJV)—"multiply on the face of the earth" (verse 1); "wickedness of man was great in the earth" (verse 5); "made man on the earth" (verse 6); "destroy man whom I have created from the face of the earth, both man and beast, creeping thing and birds of the air" (verse 7, not just herds of domesticated animals as some claim); "the earth also was corrupt before God" (verse 11, how much can God observe?); "the earth was filled with violence" (verse 11); "God looked upon the earth" (verse 12); "all flesh...on the earth" (verse 12, not just humans); "the end of all flesh" (verse 13); "the earth is filled with violence" (verse 13); "destroy them with the earth" (verse 13); "floodwaters on the earth" (verse 17); "to destroy...all flesh" (verse 17); "in which is the breath of life" (verse 17, not just domesticated animals); "from under heaven" (verse 17, not just the atmosphere above Mesopotamia); "everything that is on the earth shall die" (verse 17, animals at a distance would have been unaffected by a local flood); "every living thing of all flesh" (verse 19, couldn't just be Noah's herds); "to keep them alive" (verse 19); "birds...to keep them alive" (verse 20, birds could certainly survive a local flood).

Genesis 7 (NKJV)—"to keep the species alive" (verse 3); "on the face of all the earth" (verse 3); "all living things that I have made" (verse 4); "destroy them from the face of the earth" (verse 4); "because of the waters of the flood" (verse 7); "the waters of the flood were on the earth" (verse 10); "all the fountains" (verse 11, all, or not limited to local geysers or volcanoes); "of the great deep" (verse 11, the deep ocean); "the windows of heaven" (verse 11, a worldwide source implies a worldwide effect); "rain was on the earth" (verse 12); "forty days and forty nights" (verse 12, no local flood would do this); "every beast...all cattle" (verse 14); "every creeping thing that creeps on the earth" (verse 14, would Noah need to take rats, moles, and snakes for them to survive a local flood?); "every bird of every sort" (verse 14); "in which is the breath of life" (verse 15, applies to animals worldwide); "the waters increased" (verse 17); "lifted up the ark" (verse 17); "and it rose high above the earth" (verse 17); "waters prevailed" (verse 18, similar to a military conquest); "greatly increased" (verse 18); "on the earth" (verse 18, not just in the valley); "the surface of the waters" (verse 18, compare with the world ocean in Genesis 1:2); "the waters prevailed exceedingly" (verse 19); "on the earth" (verse 19); "all the high hills" (verse 19); "under the whole heaven" (verse 19, all that were within God's sight); "were covered" (verse 19); "fifteen cubits upward" (verse 20, the draft of the thirty-cubit Ark); "the waters prevailed" (verse 20); "the mountains were covered" (verse 20, same word in Hebrew as high hills in verse 19); "all flesh died" (verse 21); "that moved on the earth" (verse 21); "birds and cattle and beasts and every creeping thing" (verse 21); "that creeps on the earth" (verse 21, most animals are small creeping things); "on the earth" (verse 21); "and every man" (verse 21); "all in whose nostrils was the breath of life" (verse 22, all air-breathing animals); "all that was on the dry land" (verse 22); "He destroyed all living things" (verse 23); "on the face of the ground" (verse 23); "both man and cattle, creeping thing and bird of the air" (verse 23); "they were destroyed from the earth" (verse 23); "only Noah...remained alive" (verse 23); "and those who were with him in the ark" (verse 23); "the waters prevailed on the earth" (verse 24).

Genesis 8 (NKJV)—"every living thing" (verse 1); "all the animals" (verse 1); "a wind to pass over the earth" (verse 1), "the waters subsided" (verse 1); "the fountains of the deep" (verse 2); "the windows of heaven" (verse 2); "were also stopped" (verse 2); "the rain from heaven was restrained" (verse 2, a special rain, not a local storm, because those continue); "the waters receded continually" (verse 3); "from the earth" (verse 3); "the waters decreased" (verse 3); "the mountains of Ararat" (verse 4, the entire Ararat region is about one mile in elevation, the headwaters of Mesopotamian rivers; the Ark would need to float uphill in a local flood); "the waters decreased continually" (verse 5); "the tops of the mountains were seen" (verse 5, three months later); "the waters had dried up" (verse 7); "from the earth" (verse 7, after forty more days); "to see if the waters had receded" (verse 8); "from the face of the ground" (verse 8); "the dove found no resting place" (verse 9); "the waters were on the face of the whole earth" (verse 9); "the waters had receded" (verse 11); "from the earth" (verse 11); "the waters were dried up" (verse 13); "from the earth" (verse 13); "the surface of the ground" (verse 13); "the earth was dried" (verse 14); "every animal, every creeping thing, every bird, and whatever creeps on the earth" (verse 19, all of them, not some of them, left the Ark); "curse the ground" (verse 21); "every living thing" (verse 21, promise of no more such floods; couldn't be a local flood); "while the earth remains" (verse 22).

Genesis 9 (NKJV)—"Be fruitful and multiply, and fill the earth" (verse 1); "every beast of the earth" (verse 2, not just local farm animals); "every bird of the air" (verse 2); "all that move on the earth" (verse 2); "all the fish of the sea" (verse 2); "Every moving thing that lives" (verse 3); "bring forth abundantly in the earth" (verse 7); "establish My covenant" (verse 9); "with every living creature" (verse 10); "that is with you" (verse 10, all land-dwelling animals were included in this covenant); "the birds, the cattle, and every beast of the earth" (verse 10); "every beast of the earth" (verse 10); "all flesh be cut off" (verse 11); "by the waters of the flood" (verse 11); "a flood to destroy the earth" (verse 11); "every living creature" (verse 12); "perpetual generations" (verse 12); "between Me and the earth" (verse 13); "every living creature" (verse 15); "of all flesh" (verse 15); "waters shall never again become a flood" (verse 15); "to destroy all flesh" (verse 15); "every living creature" (verse 16); "of all flesh" (verse 16); "that is on the earth" (verse 16); "all flesh" (verse 17); "that is on the earth" (verse 17); "the whole earth was populated" (verse 19, today, Noah's descendants are worldwide; the same term is used to describe the Flood's extent).

ABOUT THE AUTHOR

From 1972 to 1989, Dr. John Morris traveled to Turkey more than a dozen times to look for Noah's Ark. The search for the Ark marked a turning point in his life. He was an engineer in Los Angeles and living a defeated Christian life when he turned back to God and dedicated himself to sharing biblical truth, eventually earning a PhD in geological engineering and joining the Institute for Creation Research. In his many Ararat expeditions, he witnessed abundant answers to prayer, especially preservation in times of mortal danger. He never found what he was looking for, but he and his team members did discover more about God, His nature, His power, and how they could fit into His plan. Much of Dr. Morris's experience in searching for the Ark is recorded in *Adventure on Ararat, Noah's Ark and the Ararat Adventure,* and *The Ark on Ararat* (coauthored with Dr. Tim LaHaye), articles, and presentations.

Some of his best contributions to the field of creation science have been *The Young Earth*, *The Fossil Record*, and *The Global Flood*. Drawing on Dr. Morris's extensive knowledge of geology and paleontology, these books present solid scientific evidence in support of the Genesis narrative. In them he not only demonstrates the scientific accuracy of the Bible, but also brings glory to God by showing the wonders of His creation.

Dr. Morris no longer climbs mountains or fights wild dogs, and so the search has passed on to a new generation. But the Ark still compels him, and he supports and encourages those who take up the creation cause—and he does it with the same kindness and compassion that have been staples of his character.

An Enduring Message

At ICR today, the team of scientists, scholars, and staff continues with the work of creation ministry, and ICR's message remains steady—God is faithful and His Word is true. We can be confident that true science confirms the accuracy of Scripture. And we can trust Him with the details of life—those seen and those yet to be revealed, including the biblical account of Noah's Ark.

Whether or not the Ark is ever found, there is abundant evidence of the truthfulness of God's Word. "For since the creation of the world His invisible attributes are clearly seen, being understood by the things that are made, even His eternal power and Godhead" (Romans 1:20).

For more than four decades, the Institute for Creation Research has been making "clearly seen" the truths of the Bible. And ICR will continue doing what Dr. John Morris and others before and after him have done so well—proclaiming scientific truth in creation.

Note: Some of the journal entries in this book were adapted from Dr. John Morris's *Adventure on Ararat*, Institute for Creation Research, 1973.

NOTES

1. The modern-day search for the Ark had its start with Eryl and Violet Cummings's book *Noah's Ark: Fact or Fable?*, which was a compilation of eyewitness accounts published in 1973. The book spurred a generation of "ark-eologists," the name humorously given to those who search for Noah's Ark on Mt. Ararat. I read the manuscript before it was published, and it helped turn my then-rebellious life back to Christ.

2. Adapted from Dr. John Morris's a article "Why Does Nearly Every Culture Have a Tradition of a Global Flood?" in the September 2001 edition of *Acts & Facts*.

3. John D. Morris, 2004. What Geologic Processes Were Operating During the Flood? *Acts & Facts*, 33 (9).

4. John D. Morris, "Why Did God Give the Rainbow Sign?" *Acts & Facts*, 2006, 35 (1).

5. John D. Morris, PhD, "The Search for Noah's Ark: 1983," *Acts & Facts*, 1983, 12 (11).

6. John D. Morris, *Adventure on Ararat* (San Diego: Creation-Life Publishers, 1973).

7. John D. Morris, *Ark on Ararat* (San Diego: Creation-Life Publishers, 1975).

8. Second edition note from Dr. John: This cave is known to the locals as the Cave of Saint Lawrence, named after Lawrence of Arabia of World War I fame. Lawrence was fluent in Arabic and Turkish and mainly utilized his skills to help the Allies fight the Ottoman Turks. Once the war was over and the Turks routed, Lawrence evidently had little purpose in life. But he still hated the Turks. The locals tell me that he migrated to the Kurdish territory of Mount Ararat. The Kurds had a similar animosity toward the Turks. Lawrence and his assistant took up residence in this cave on Mount Ararat, and he portrayed himself as a "holy man." Old men of the area tell me he smeared phosphorous on his face so it would glow. He told the locals that he was so holy he did not need food. But they did notice that the assistant ate enough for two. He taught the locals that when the time was right they would rebel against the Turks and overcome them. When that time came, they attacked with pitchforks, farming implements, and little else. The Turks had modern military weapons and easily repelled them. Lawrence vanished. The only evidence for this story is the memory of elderly Kurds and the old Cave of Saint Lawrence in the Ahora Gorge. Even today, the Kurds still oppose the Turks.

9. In addition to the two J.D. Morris books mentioned in notes 6 and 7, see V. Cummings, *Has Anybody Really Seen Noah's Ark?* (San Diego: Creation-Life Publishers, 1982).

10. John D. Morris, "A Report on the ICR Ararat Expedition, 1987," *Acts & Facts*, 1987, 17 (1).

11. John D. Morris, PhD, "The Search for Noah's Ark: Status 1992," *Acts & Facts*, 1992, 21 (9).

DINOSAURS
AND THE BIBLE

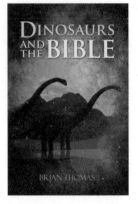

- When and where did dinosaurs live?
- Are they mentioned in the Bible?
- What does the fossil evidence tell us about them?

Some people say dinosaurs lived many millions of years ago, long before humans inhabited the earth. The Bible says that on Day Six of creation, God made the animals that live on land, as well as man and woman.

So where do dinosaurs fit in?

Dinosaurs and the Bible explores the scientific, historical, scriptural, and fossil evidence about dinosaurs and shares what we can know after many years of thoughtful, careful research.